How to Build a House

A Practical, Common-Sense Guide to Residential Construction

GEORGE MICHAEL RENTZ, PE

iUniverse, Inc.
Bloomington

How to Build a House
A Practical, Common-Sense Guide to Residential Construction

iUniverse books may be ordered through booksellers or by contacting:

iUniverse
1663 Liberty Drive
Bloomington, IN 47403
www.iuniverse.com
1-800-Authors (1-800-288-4677)

ISBN: 978-1-4502-8861-3 (pbk)
ISBN: 978-1-4502-8860-6 (cloth)
ISBN: 978-1-4502-9029-6 (ebk)

Library of Congress Control Number: 2011900424

Printed in the United States of America

iUniverse rev. date: 3/18/11

CONTENTS

INTRODUCTION

Over the years, I have been asked many questions by people involved with all aspects of the residential housing industry, including homeowners and contractors. I am writing this book as an answer to those questions and to assist people who have minimal knowledge about the residential housing industry and are planning to build a house. It will also be of help if you're going to buy a house and wonder how it all came together. For the purposes of this book, the residential housing industry means the blue- and white-collar professionals and their respected residential construction industries. Also, this book may benefit those people who have knowledge of these industries and yet wish to get involved. For those of you who have limited knowledge about these residential professionals, they usually will tell you that they have forgotten more about building houses than you will ever know.

The PE after my name stands for professional engineer. In order to practice engineering legally, you have to become licensed by the state you're practicing in. I was originally licensed in South Carolina in 1982, and I am now licensed in fourteen states. To become licensed, you have to graduate from an accredited university and then pass an eight-hour test to become an EIT (engineer in training). Then you have to work for a minimum of four years in responsible charge under a licensed engineer. After that, you have to have five licensed engineers sign for you, a statement that you know what's what. Then you take another eight-hour test, and if you pass it, you're a professional engineer. If everything goes right, it takes a minimum of nine years to become a professional engineer. To me, engineering is nothing more than common sense applied to mathematics. Let's say you wanted to build a bridge across a river. Anyone could do it; just fill the river up with concrete. An engineer should be able to do it a lot less expensively and a lot safer than that—and that's why we know what's what.

I've enjoyed building things since I was a kid, and I've always been good with math. I grew up in rural South Carolina, and like all country boys, I learned to use tools at a young age. There was a sawmill in Loris, the town I grew up in, and I lived near Mr. Watkins, the man who owned it. He let me have all the scrap lumber I could carry. I built a lot of tree houses, clubhouses, and underground forts. I had to get my own nails, so I would pick up bent nails at construction sites and straighten them. By the way, the best way to do that is to put the nail in the concave mortar joint on your front steps, letting the head stick past the edge of the brick, and carefully hammer the nail straight.

I started the great University of South Carolina in 1970, majoring in philosophy, and dropped out after a year. I worked in various construction jobs until 1974 when I returned to USC in engineering. I graduated in civil engineering in 1977. I built my first house for my father in 1977 and then went to work with Kline Iron and Steel for four years. After Kline, I worked for an A/E firm and two construction companies. I started my own structural engineering firm in 1985. My son graduated from the great USC in 2010 with a degree in civil engineering, and perhaps I can retire soon.

Being involved with the design and construction of your own house is one of the most difficult, time-consuming, and trying life experiences a person can go through. It matters not if you have built many houses for yourself; even if you think you've seen it all, something new will surprise you. An architect who assisted me with my last house said that when couples hire him, he tells them that almost every couple that goes through the construction of their dream house winds up going to a marriage counselor or getting divorced! My wife and I made it through the construction of our dream house, so it can be done. There are many good and bad times involved with house construction. Hopefully, this book will assist you in having more good times than bad, and the construction of your own single-family dwelling will be a rewarding, enjoyable experience.

If you are not a residential contractor and you want to build your own house without a contractor, come to your senses. I would suggest that you try to build a car first; if you succeed, you may be able to build a house. Most of the people who try to be their own contractor think they're going to save money. If they knew how many legitimate contractors sometimes don't see a profit on a house, they would not be so foolish. Don't think you can work at your regular job and build a house on the side. Don't think that all the subcontractors that you're going to need are going to stop work with their year-round contractors just to come work on your one house. Don't think you can build a house cheaper than someone who's set up in a business to build houses. Find someone who has tried to be his own contractor and ask if they would do it again. The best advice I can give these people is to save their money, time, and heartburn and hire a good residential contractor. Remember, they have forgotten more than you will ever know about house building.

The table of contents in this book is listed in a chronological order of events that I would follow to build a house. Some people will change the order, and that's fine with me, but you cannot eliminate any of the items discussed in any of the chapters. All of them are important in building a house. All of the items discussed in the chapters are my opinion of what I would do if I were going to live in the house. When it comes to aesthetics, you and I may not like the same thing or think the same things are pretty. Use your judgment when it comes to what you like in your own house.

Chapter 1

Site and House Planning and Design

Aerial picture of house and site

The patch of planet Earth the house will sit on is the *house site*. The site includes the geographic location—where on the planet you are—and the specific physical characteristics of the earth under and surrounding the house.

The geographic location of the site includes the following considerations:

- ✓ Are you in the northern or southern hemisphere? If you don't know, in the northern hemisphere, hurricane winds blow counterclockwise and water goes down the toilet counterclockwise. In the southern hemisphere, it is the opposite.
- ✓ In this hemisphere, are you near the equator or the poles or in the middle?
- ✓ Generally, what is the climate where your house will be built?
- ✓ What is the yearly rainfall? How much rain is in the hundred-year, twenty-four-hour storm?
- ✓ What is the average monthly temperature, including hottest and coldest months?
- ✓ What is the average humidity?
- ✓ What is the yearly amount of snow and the design snow load?
- ✓ How deep is the frost action in the ground?
- ✓ What is the highest wind speed and from what direction?
- ✓ Is the house located in an earthquake-prone zone?

All of these items must be addressed in the design of the house.

Specific characteristics of the site include the following considerations:

- ✓ Are there roads to the site?
- ✓ Is electric power already there, or will you need to use mobile electric generators until power is brought to the site by the utility company?
- ✓ Are potable (drinking) water and sewer services already there, or do you need a well and a septic tank with drain fields? If you need a septic tank, what is the percolation rate for the soil? If you have sewer service, is it gravity flow or do you need a pump station?
- ✓ Is the site high and dry on good, firm soil, or is it in a low lying wet area with loose, fluid soil?
- ✓ Is the site flat, or is the site on a hill or mountain or steep slope or cliff?

 ✓ Is the soil solid rock, rocky, sandy, clay, quicksand, or a combination?
 ✓ Is the site on a lake or ocean or body of water or in the middle of a big city?
 ✓ Is the site in a subdivision with covenants that dictate the type and size of the house and use of the land?

These site characteristics impact the construction cost and time, and the future maintenance of the house.

Choosing the Best Site for Your House

Choosing the best site for your house can be done in two ways. First, do you already know what type of house you want (Spanish, farm, townhouse, etc.) and just need a site to build on? Will any site do as long as you can make it fit the house? Second, do you know what area you want to live in (ocean, mountains, city, subdivision, country), and will you design the house to fit the site (kind of like site-specific art)? I recommend that you choose the area you want to live in and match the house to the site. You still have certain types of houses you like but aren't dead-set on a specific one and nothing else. You're flexible—and they say that's always good, unless you're trying to row a rowboat with a rope. Unless the site you pick is so unrelated to the type of house you like, matching the house to the site is the best way to go. Keep in mind, however, that a New York City townhouse on the top of a peak in the Rocky Mountains just doesn't seem right.

Access to the site is the only thing some people think about when it comes to site considerations. What are the directions to the house? Directions to some houses in the sticks will usually include something like "Turn off the paved road just past the dumpster," but there's more to site access than directions. First, be sure there is a road to the site that can handle construction traffic, such as concrete trucks and building supply trucks. If you have to build a road (not a driveway) to get to your site, you will need to find another source for information. Road construction is a topic separate from residential construction and is not discussed in this book, except to say that relative to the cost of houses, roads are very expensive to build and maintain. If you have to build a road, don't let some levelheaded bulldozer operator talk you into letting him cut your road in for you so he can save you some money. If the chewing tobacco drips from both sides of his mouth at the same time, you know he's levelheaded. In that case, just tell him that when you want to chew some horse dung, you'll let him know. Go hire a civil engineer to design the road and supervise the construction.

Some roads are not designed for highway loads (such as tractor-trailers) and can be seriously damaged by construction traffic. Some roads are too steep for construction traffic, and the construction material will have to be offloaded at the base of a hill and double handled with four-wheel drive forklifts to get to the top. Some sites don't have roads at all. Island sites without bridges will have to use boats and barges to get the construction material to the house site. Sites without proper access for construction material will increase the cost of the construction and the time it takes to build.

Water

The above mentioned questions involving the forces of nature (wind, rain, snow, etc.) for a general area are easily answered by the local building officials and codes and the design professionals (architect, engineers, and contractors). The physical characteristics of the specific site require a little more understanding. This brings me to one of the most important topics a person needs to understand about residential construction: water. You may think I'm getting off the site topic, but bear with me. Water is such an important topic that some aspect of it needs to be addressed now.

I know water sounds kind of simple, and it is, but it's also very important. Ninety percent of all the problems I've seen in houses have involved water. These problems could have been avoided with a little understanding and planning. If you don't think water can cause problems, just try to breathe it.

On earth, water runs downhill and follows the path of least resistance. I think the part about water running downhill was the basis for several doctoral programs at a major university; I could be wrong though. Water flowing at ten miles per hour is approximately equal to the force of wind blowing at a hundred miles per hour. Water is the universal solvent; given enough time, it will dissolve anything. Running water usually purifies itself. Fresh water weights 62.2 pounds per cubic foot, and saltwater weights 64.4 pounds per cubic foot. Water is the only liquid that expands when it freezes. Water is made of hydrogen and oxygen, both highly flammable, yet water does not burn. Cool water on a hot day is one of life's sweet pleasures. Life as we know it on earth, or anywhere else, cannot be sustained very long without water. These are just some of the properties of H2O that we will expand on later.

Water is one of the most important things to plan for when designing a house. To keep it simple, water is good and bad. To give you an example of the good use of water, consider the location of water outlets in the house. There are sinks, tubs, showers, dishwashers, water heaters, icemakers, refrigerators, drinking fountains, washing machines, steam machines, humidifiers, exterior wall faucets, pools, exterior fountains, hot tubs, irrigation, condensation lines, toilets, and the list goes on. People normally associate these water outlets with good feelings, and they should.

Water becomes bad (in fact downright mean) when it is not planned for or is allowed to go uncontrolled in and around a house—for example, water leaks. Leaks occur in pipes, roofs, basements, windows, doors, pools, etc. Just about any place where there is water, it can leak if not controlled. Have you ever tried to find a leak in a roof? Keep in mind that water flows downhill, so where you see the leak coming through the ceiling is usually not where its source is. It's somewhere uphill. Storm water surface runoff and underground water can cause major problems for a house if not controlled. If a house is on a body of water, storm surges and flooding can destroy a house very quickly. Water in the form of snow or ice can collapse a roof. Pipes can freeze and burst. Termites cannot live without water, and mold and fungus cannot grow. Wherever there is an introduction point for water, there must be a discharge point. If there is no discharge point and if the water does not evaporate, it may become stagnant and breed mosquitoes. Water can be really nasty if we allow it to be.

Preventing water from becoming a problem during the life of the house is one of the most important parts of the house and site plan. The areas involving water need careful thought. When proportioning the money to be spent on the various items in the house, do not skimp on the ones involving water. Some typical areas where water can become a problem are roof flashing, gutters, toilets, sinks, water heaters, and anything water is piped to or rain can get to.

I have witnessed many times when people think they're saving money by stopping the tile around the shower just above the showerhead and installing wallpaper or paint from the top of the tile to the ceiling. Any savings in the initial cost of the tile is quickly lost when the wallpaper or paint peels off the wall and mildew grows due to the moisture from the shower. This becomes a maintenance problem and will continue to get worse until the tile is run up to the ceiling.

A second major problem area for water is roofs. One of the dumbest things ever conceived by the construction industry is the concept of flat roofs. These roofs leak and never stop. If not designed stiff enough, they also do a thing called *ponding*. Flat roofs are supposed to have scuppers four inches or so above the low point in the roof. Most of them do, but the designer forgot to tell the leaves not to clog up the scuppers. Ponding is a situation in a flat roof where the water cannot run off. As the depth of water on the roof increases, the water's weight makes the members sag. When they sag, they make a little pond. The little pond can hold more water, so there's more sag, then more water, then more sag, and so on until everyone involved with the roof gives you their best surprised look—that is, if nobody got hurt.

The third problem area is storm drainage. I have seen houses that have downspouts that empty the storm water directly by the exterior wall of the house and make no previsions for it to drain off. Over time, the soil around the downspout becomes saturated from the water and loses its bearing capacity. Basically the soil turns to mud, and the foundations sink in this area, cracking everything above them.

These are just three of the things this book will help you avoid; we will cover others later on. Where all of the water comes from and goes to in a house must be thought out. If not, you may hear those dripping sounds in the night that remind you of what you read in this book.

We'll get back to water inside the house later in the book. For now, with regard to the site, let's look at how all the water that will come into contact with the site should be addressed.

When it rains, where will the storm water run? Will water from adjacent sites or the street run to your site? When you place your house on the site will you dam the natural runoff of the water? The ideal site for surface runoff or flooding would be one where the house location is, also the highest point in the site. This location would prevent water from running toward the house, and the water from the roof would run away from the house. If the house location is not at the highest elevation on the site, then some water will flow toward the house and must be diverted around the house. This is done with grading the surface with swells (swells are wide, flat ditches) and installing drains around the perimeter of the house.

If your site is on a body of water, you will have to know the high water mark. Some people call this the *high* high water mark because when the moon is in a certain location, the water is higher on site than normal high water. If your site has tide ranges, you need to know high tide and low tide and storm surge elevations. If you are on a river, you will need to know the hundred-year flood stages. On your specific site, there is an elevation to which the water is not supposed to rise; that's the high water mark. The living space in the house has to be above this elevation, and the remaining structure must be designed for the moving water if it can come in contact with the house.

These high water marks are measured from the elevation of the oceans. If the elevation for your house on your site is 360 feet MSL (mean sea level), this means that the house must be 360 feet above the mean sea level of the ocean. Your site may be 350 feet MSL, in which case your house would be ten feet higher than your site. These numbers vary from site to site and really only come into play if you are on a body of water or in a floodplain. If you are on a body of water, your house must be designed for the worst-case scenario of the water from a hundred-year storm. Designing a house to withstand flowing water is extremely expensive; keep that in mind if your site is on a body of water. If your site is on a body of water, it is usually on the downhill side of the surrounding sites. When a rainstorm comes, a lot of water will run through your site to the body of water.

Most sites are not involved with a body of water. However, a hundred-year rainstorm (or snowstorm when it melts) can produce a lot of water. For example, say the hundred-year storm in your area was seven inches of rain in twenty-four hours. A 10,000 square foot lot, (100 feet times 100 feet), or approximately a one-quarter acre lot, would produce 43,633 gallons of water if all the rain ran off the site. One inch of rain would produce 6,233 gallons of water over the site. If the house on the site is 2,500 square feet, the amount of water that would fall on the house in the hundred-year storm would be 10,908 gallons in twenty-four hours. Again, one inch would be 1,558 gallons. Unless the roof leaks, all of this water is going to run off the house. All of the water on the nonporous areas like patios, driveways, and streets is going to run off somewhere. If your site has the type of soil, such as sand or a granular type soil, that will allow water to soak into the ground, that's good as long as it doesn't soak into the ground around the perimeter of the house.

Some soils are very porous, and others are not. The perk test tells how fast water soaks into the ground (so many gallons per hour). Perk tests are required for septic tank permits. How fast the water soaks into the ground (perks) will determine how long the drain lines have to be for the septic tank or if you can have a septic system at all. The best way to see where and what the storm water will do on your site is to visit it during a heavy rain and watch your site and the surrounding ones. If the water does not soak into the ground quickly enough, manholes and piping may be required to drain the site. One way to determine how quickly the water needs to soak into the ground is to decide how long you want to look at a puddle of water in your yard. During a frog-drowning storm, say five inches of rain an hour, I would be happy if the water was gone by the next morning. The last thing you want is for the surrounding sites or streets to drain through your site. If there is a storm water easement running through your site, be wary. Even if the easement is piped underground with manholes, pipes clog up sooner or later, and there are always maintenance problems. If the pipes clog, what will the water do on your site?

The water table is the depth from ground surface down to where water is found in the soil. If you need a well on your site, you will have to know this. How deep the water table is determines how much the well will cost. Water tables vary greatly, from ground surface at the ocean and in swampy areas to several hundred feet deep in the mountains and in deserts. A high water table will impact the foundation or basement of the house and the driveway and roads. This is because when soil gets wet, it loses some of its bearing capacity, so the foundation will have to get bigger. Water tables on sites near bodies of water are usually at the surface elevation of the water and vary with the seasons and elevation of the water. I do not recommend putting a basement in a house if the basement will be below the water table. Even if the basement is "waterproofed" and there is a sump pump in the basement floor, the basement will leak and the sump pump will wear out.

There are things called perched water tables; these are lenses of water that are trapped at different levels in the soil. Usually you can punch through them with a drill rig and they will drain; or you can open one end and they will drain. These are usually found in hilly, rocky soil, but they can be in any nonporous soil. Unless you are in a remote area, the water table is usually known for most areas where humans live. If you need a water well on your site, you can check with the surrounding houses closest to your site to find out the information on the water table. Good information would be how many gallons a minute is available. This is determined by how fast the water flows through the soil and how fast you can pump it out with a certain size well. Whether the water is hard or soft and how it tastes is also useful information. Sometimes there is water available at a certain elevation and better water at a deeper depth. The local well driller usually knows all about this type of information, but I would still talk with the neighbors closest to the site. Bad information would be that the water is very deep; you can't get enough gallons per minute, so you will need a large reservoir and you will have to treat it to use it. This is rare unless you are on some islands in the ocean where the only drinking water comes from the rain and must be stored in cisterns and purified.

I think by now you can see how important water is to the design and construction of your house. Be sure that you know where the water comes from and where it's going before you pick your site or build your house.

Utilities

Once you're aware of the water issues specific to your site, you need to check out a few other things, like the utilities that you'll need in your house. Where are the utility taps located on the site, and how much are the tap fees? Are the utilities underground or on poles? Who is responsible for the common utilities, such as streetlights and fire hydrants, if there are any?

Utilities include electricity, phones, gas, water, sewer, cable, etc. The utility taps are the locations where the utility companies stop their lines and the homeowners start theirs. The water and sewer lines taps are usually at the property lines and are normally underground. The sewer line tap is usually on the downhill side of the site. The cost of running the water and sewer from the tap to the house is usually the homeowner's responsibility. The electricity, phones, gas, and cable utilities are usually run to the house by the utility company. These are either buried or run overhead on poles. Sometimes there's a charge for running the utilities from the property line to the house. If the site is large or the soil is rocky or hilly and hard to dig, the charge can get very large. Usually if the utilities are running overhead, you can pay the utility company extra to put them underground. Before the utilities are run to your house, be sure to work out with the utility companies where and how they are going to run the lines. They will want to run the lines the least expensive way for them. This may involve cutting down some of your favorite trees on your site. If you don't work out the details, it may surprise you when the utility company's crews arrive with chainsaws.

The above information is easy to obtain from a licensed professional land surveyor. When you buy your site, you will have to get a boundary line survey. This survey will give the legal description of the property. It should show all the property lines, easements, utilities, tap locations, flood ways, and all physical aspects of the property. It should also show the elevation above sea level at one of the corners of the property, but sometimes it doesn't. When you get the boundary line survey, you can have the trees located and the topographic contours shown on the survey. I recommend that the topo and trees be shown on a separate drawing. It is best to have surveys done when the line of sight is clear. This would be in the winter when the leaves have fallen. It would be very expensive to have all the trees located, so most surveys only locate trees over six inches in diameter. You can select what size trees you want located. If the site is hilly, the topo will take longer and be more expensive, but it becomes even more necessary in the design of the site and house.

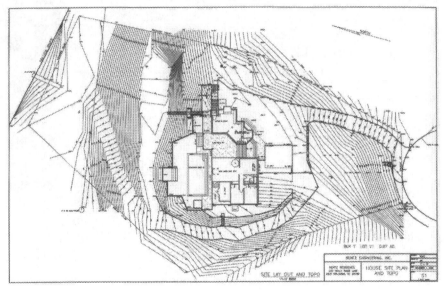

Figure 1. Topo of the site in the aerial photo at the beginning of chapter 1

Boundary Line Survey

Okay, you kind of know what type of house you want, you have settled on a beautiful site, and you're ready to buy it. You or your real estate agent have made sure that it's not in the future or present flight path of the local jet port or next to a train track or some future chicken processing plant or hog farm or metal recycling plant or anything that may detract from the peace and quiet and environmental pureness in your new home.

When you buy this property, the deed will need a legal description of the property on it, and you will need a registered professional land surveyor for that. The state where your site is located should have some type of State Board of Registration for professional engineers, architects, and land surveyors, and they should have a roster of registered professional land surveyors that you can choose from. Or, you may know a contractor or an architect or engineer that can recommend one to you. You meet with the registered professional land surveyor and you tell him something like the following:

"I'm going to buy this piece of property, and I need a survey for my deed. I know I probably could get by with the bare minimum legal description for my deed, but on my survey I want the following information clearly shown and drawn to a reasonable scale (hopefully something around one inch equals ten feet on a 24 x 36-inch paper)."

> *Note: A large site will require a much smaller scale. Keep in mind that a boundary line survey at a small scale on a small 11 x 17-inch paper may be fine for the deed to the property but will have to be redrawn to the same scale as the house is drawn in order to be useful with the house plans.*

- Show the location of the site relative to the nearest town, city, or county of the governing building department that has jurisdiction over the site, showing the roads to scale that lead to the site from the nearest state highway.
- Show any existing buildings or structures, property lines with dimension, streets, easements, and setbacks.
- Show all water, sewer, electrical, phone, gas, TV, cable, and utilities coming to the site, including the location of the nearest fire hydrant connection.
- Show the size of the site with the boundary lines shown in length and direction from magnetic north, along with a magnetic north arrow.
- Show all of the utility taps, including but not limited to drinking water, sanitary sewer, storm sewer, gas, electricity, cable TV, phones, utility and storm easements locations. They are to be clearly defined, including approximate depth below

ground surface, and shown along with all pertinent flood or high water control lines.

- Show any requirements as to the elevation of the first habitable floor of any residence on the site and any height restriction or number of story restrictions.
- Show any utility poles or underground lines.
- A benchmark referenced from mean sea level shall be established and noted with a monument or some permanent method, and contour lines not to exceed 5' on center vertically are to be shown on the plan.

Note: An iron pipe driven into the ground with the top set at a certain elevation is not a good method for establishing a benchmark. It's too easy for some disgruntled person, or some MIT graduate that thinks the C in Clemson stands for knowledge, to walk by the pipe every day and hit it with his hammer so that the benchmark changes every day and only he knows it, just so he can watch the house go up out of level while the contractor that could have graduated from Clemson scratches his head and gives you that dreaded surprised look. Usually a manhole lid or something made of concrete that is very difficult to move is used as a benchmark. Everything in the house can be measured in the vertical direction from the benchmark. The benchmark is the best way to start level and stay level throughout the construction of the house, and we all want our floors to be level.

- Show all trees over six inch in diameter *(or whatever you wish, depending on your persuasion with regard to cutting down trees).*

Note: Keep in mind that trees that are left in place and have their roots cut when building the foundations usually die as soon as the contractor is no longer responsible for them. So now, this grand old gentleman of a hickory tree that you did not have the heart to cut down died, and the no-good sucker fell right through the roof at two o'clock in the morning during a bad rainstorm, and you know it just had to happen on your daughter's wedding day, and you know the contractor is invited to the wedding, and you know he told you so. Anyway, you have a tree surgeon come in and take down some trees that may do the same thing, like the one that you built the wood deck around and diverted the rain from the roots. It's dying, and the tree surgeon tells you he can't take it down without a crane or he may damage your house because the tree is too close to the house. So you tell him to bring in the crane, and the crane cracks the hell out of the concrete driveway and the underground sewer line. Keep in mind that the trees need careful planning, along with your landscaping, but we will get to that.

• All of the corners are to be marked with an iron rod. A legal description of the property is to be noted on the survey along with all information required by the governing regulatory authorities regarding the site, including setback lines and environmental controls during construction and all other site-specific regulatory requirements.

Finally, ask for two originals and six copies of the survey sealed and signed by the registered professional land surveyor.

Depending on how readily available the above information is, the workload of the surveyor, and your time schedule, you may wish to talk to several surveyors before you decide on one. Sites in a developed subdivision should have all of this information already gathered in the subdivision layout plans; therefore, the cost should be less than that of one in an undeveloped area. Agree to a fixed price and time frame in writing with the surveyor you choose prior to the surveyor beginning any work. There should be many qualified surveyors that can do this work, so just pick the one you like, as long as he is qualified for this type of work and licensed. Don't use the one who tells you that you don't need all of this information. If you are already using a homebuilder or architect, etc., they may include the survey you will need with the house.

The idea is that you will need all of the above information at some time during the planning and construction and future of the house. It is much better to get the information from the start than to have to stop work while the needed information is obtained. Also, the location of the house on the site can be optimized by knowing the proposed utility service routes and existing utilities on the site, the available parking and construction lay down areas, and drainage and grading information with reference to finished first floors and adjacent streets and other houses or vistas.

The final location of all the underground utilities that are run to your house should be located on this survey as soon as they are installed so that there is an accurate location of these lines. This will help several years from now when you're planting some nice new trees with three-feet root balls far away from your house, so it will be pretty, and you've hired some of the local high school football players to dig the holes and tote the trees. You won't anger your neighbors and your friends by accidentally cutting the cable TV line the day before the Super Bowl party at your house, which is why you needed to have the dumb trees planted anyway.

Site and House Plans

After you have bought the property, you have to determine how to grade it so that the house and site work as one. Now it is time, if you haven't already done so, to hire a professional who's experienced in residential construction to help you with the plans for your house and site. This could be in the form of an architect or engineer experienced in developing house plans. Or, there are specific companies, while not architectural firms, that have considerable experience in residential work and do a really good job of developing house and site plans. Some residential contractors also have divisions within their company that can provide you with plans, and they also do a really good job. The point is it's time to join the house with the site. The way to do that is with studying, drawings, and more studying and more drawings, as you will see by the time you finish this book.

Keep this in mind when choosing whom you are going to hire to develop your house and site plans. You want someone who is required to be licensed by the state where you are building your house. Some states do not require persons that just draw house plans to be licensed, while they do require homebuilders and architects and engineers to be licensed. If the professional you hire to develop your house and site plans is licensed by the state, there is some avenue of recourse through the licensing body if some dispute should arise. Although a dispute with a professional is rare, they do occur and the licensing boards have ways to resolve them. Personally, I would recommend that you use the services of an architect with many years of experience in residential construction. Whomever you use, be sure that they have many years of design and drafting experience in residential construction.

Codes

Above, I mentioned regulatory requirements. That's a fancy way to say building codes. Throughout this book, I will describe codes by different words and phrases. This is because there are a lot of different codes. The building codes that apply to the house you are building will depend on what codes the local building officials have adopted in the area you are building in. There are national, state, county, and city codes that may govern the construction of your house. Over the last few years, these codes have evolved into a code called the International Residential Building Code. If the area you are building in has adopted it, then that code and all the codes it refers you to will be the regulatory requirements.

Over time, some very notable construction has been built without the use of codes—structures like the Taj Mahal, St. Michael's, the Eiffel Tower, the Hoover Dam, the Brooklyn Bridge, and a whole lot of houses. Some things in the code make no sense to me, but the overall intent of the code is good. They say it's necessary to ensure that you have a nice, safe house. Since the general public cannot just walk into your house, the residential codes are not as stringent as the codes for buildings used by the general public. However, in my opinion, residential codes are dealing more and more with how you live rather than what the structure is all about. In the sixties, there were no residential codes to speak of. Now the IBC residential code and all its references are several inches thick. No builder likes to hear the dreaded words "code violation," so most builders are up to snuff on the regulatory requirements that govern the areas they build in.

In most areas, before you can begin building your house, you must get a building permit from the local governing building department. This usually involves taking your plans to them, giving them some money, waiting a few days while the plans go through plan review, and then getting a building permit. If you have an ugly set of plans, get ready to deal with the bureaucrats. If you have a pretty set of plans, there is usually no problem getting a permit. Whatever you do, try not to get these officials mad at you. They will be inspecting your house during construction, and you cannot move in until they give you a CO (Certificate of Occupancy). So be nice for goodness sake; they are only protecting you from yourself, and most of them are nice and do a good job.

One other thing: The codes have requirements about how, when, and where you have to post this building permit on your building site. If you do not post this permit correctly, that's a code violation.

Figure 2. Elevation plans of house and site

Grading

Grading the site simply means changing the existing ground surface of the site to fit the new driveway, roads, yards, gardens, pools, house and outbuildings, etc. This can be simple or complex, inexpensive or a major cost. If the site is flat with no trees, all you need to do is install the foundations and you are on your way. Usually, the site will not be flat, and there will be trees, and you will need a piece of heavy equipment like the infamous bulldozer.

First, we decide where the house and everything involved with it are going to go on the site and exactly where we want the bulldozers to go—and more importantly, where not to let one square inch of that cold, steel track run over your pretty, sweet ground. Most likely, there will be dirt that will have to be moved around. How this dirt is moved around is called *grading the site*. Where the dirt (some people like to call it soil or earth) is moved is where the trees will disappear. The trick to grading the site is to do it only once, so this will require a plan and someone who can read it. Grading a site should never be done with the naked eye. It must be done with transits and levels and measuring rods and tapes and grade stakes. The footprint and location of the house is measured from the property lines. The elevation of the batter boards (first floor) is taken from the benchmark. The locations on the ground surface to determine the amount of dirt to be moved around is also shot from the benchmark. With the proper plans, the site can be balanced or get as close to balanced as possible. All of this means that you will not need to haul any dirt onto the site and you will not need to haul any dirt off the site. All the dirt that's cut away will be used to fill the areas where the dirt is needed, and everything will be balanced out.

When all of this is done, you should have a nice, level area for the house to sit on with a driveway leading to it. The site should get shaped by those bulldozers so that when it rains, the surface water runs away from the house and to some place that is designed for it. You now have a front and back yard and are just about ready for landscaping. All the trees that you wanted to save are still there. Accomplishing this will have involved some study on the part of your design professional and a detailed site plan showing the new grade contours relative to the existing grade contours, shown on the drawing done by the registered professional land surveyor.

Letting the dozer operator have a free hand on your property to do as he pleases will leave you flattened. The good ones will ask for the grading plan they are to follow. They know this is the best way to go. You can tell how good the dozer operator is by the way the equipment looks on the trailer and the way he unloads the equipment from the trailer it is on. If there is a buildup of mud and dirt on and around the tracks, you know the equipment was not cleaned and greased from the last job. Most intelligent people take care of an expensive piece of equipment like a dozer. If your streets are paved and he unloads the dozer on the street and gouges a hole in the pavement with the dozer's steel tracks right in front of your new house and on your neighbor's street, and you have to look at that hole until the street is repaved, you know the guy doesn't care. If he offloads where he can do no damage, you usually can be sure he is experienced enough to know that he will have to leave his equipment overnight and he wants the people that are there to be his friends and watch out for his stuff. He'll probably be conscientious and do a good job. Just be sure the person that offloads the equipment right is the same one that operates it on your property. Also be sure you speak the same language, or you'll find out that that dumb, surprised look is universal. If he gives you any trouble, just have one of your neighbor's young sons go over and say something like this to the operator: "Hey, mister, if you give me a dollar, I'll watch your equipment tonight and be sure nobody tries to start it and use it to fix that hole in the road you made." He'll usually get the message.

Remember, if the bulldozer runs over you twice, you can't learn, so be sure everything you expect to see when the grading is finished is real clear with the owner of the dozer before the dozer even pulls up to the site. If you get the chance, operating a dozer for even just a few seconds is a really cool feeling of power; however, when you need to talk to the person doing the site work, it is best if you ask for the equipment to be turned off just so you can hear. And remember, just because the equipment is running around in a circle does not mean any work is being done, even if it looks and sounds like it is. For my friends in the legal profession, it is not recommended to try to serve legal papers to a dozer operator while he is running the equipment.

Chapter 2

Foundations

The foundations of a typical house are usually the least expensive and least complex part of the construction of the house, while at the same time they are the most important. When the work begins on the foundations, there is usually no other trade working on the house, so the foundation contractor has the whole site to himself and no one gets in his way. The materials for the foundations, usually concrete and steel reinforcing rods, are inexpensive compared to other material used in the house. The foundation work for a typical house usually is as simple as digging ditches or holes in the ground and laying in reinforcing rods (rebar) and placing concrete to the desired elevations.

The foundations for a non-typical house can become very complex and very expensive. A non-typical house would be one that requires deep foundations like piles or caissons or the like. These types of houses are located on very poor soil conditions where the foundations have to penetrate through bad soil to get to a good layer or are at locations where the livable first floor must be up above the existing grade for water or other requirements, such as parking. A non-typical house would be one on the ocean shore line where the house needs to be above storm surge levels and there are high winds, or in a swamp or low area where the upper levels of the soil are not strong enough to support the house. We will touch on non-typical foundations a little later.

Typical house foundations are made of concrete and rebar, and the bottom of the foundations should be deep enough in the ground so that they are below the frost line depth for the part of the country the house is being built in. The top of the foundations should be deep enough below the ground surface so that vegetation can grow say around eight inches minimum. Frost action is where the water in the soil freezes and expands and can lift or move whatever is supported by the soil. Frost action is a few inches in the south of the United States to several feet in the north. The local building official can tell you what the depth of the foundations needs to be for frost action.

In the north, where it is several feet, it is usually more economical to build a basement with the house because you have to go so deep with the foundations anyway. There are other ways to stop frost action, such as heating the soil or building the foundations on gravel beds with a French drain type of system so that the water drains away and there is none to freeze. I do not recommend this for houses because they involve too much maintenance, and it usually is much more economical to place the foundation below the frost action depth. What all this means is that the foundations go underground, never to be seen again, so get them right the first time, and hopefully you never will see them again. If you have to dig them up, it will not be fun, and it will be expensive.

The foundation for a house is supposed to do one thing and that is to transfer the loads from the house to the ground in such a way that the house appears not to move. I say appears not to move because all houses move. This movement is usually so slight that humans cannot perceive it, and most of the movement usually occurs during construction. Houses move because the soil is elastic and has voids in it. This being the case, you will get movement with the elasticity of the soil, and you will get consolidation settlements as the voids are mashed out. If the foundations are not properly designed to transfer the loads to the ground, the foundation will fail and you will get large movements and/or differential settlements. You don't want either of these.

I hope that word "loads" caught your attention. It is just another word for the weight of the house, everything in it, and everything that can push against or move it.

We design professionals like to use big words like that. Some people call the loads *forces*; they are the same thing. These loads are categorized into dead loads, live loads, wind loads, seismic loads—and if you build in the water, there would be current or wave loads. If you have an elevator or a helicopter-landing pad on the roof, there would be impact loads. If you have a basement, there would be backfill loads. I think you get the picture. These loads all have to get transferred to the ground with the foundations.

I am going to try to explain these loads in a little more detail, so bear with me on this.

Loads

Dead loads are the weight of everything that is attached permanently to the house. Basically this is the weight of the house with all of its construction material. The weight of these construction materials is well known; thus the dead load of a house can be calculated very accurately.

The *live loads* are everything that is not attached permanently to the house but will be in it or on it. *Live loads* would be the people in the house (think parties), the furniture, the file cabinets, the helicopter on the roof, the house plants, the pool table, the exercise weight machines, the water beds, the sculpture, the fish tanks, the stuff in the attic, snow or ice on the roofs, and it goes on and on. It is everything and everybody that you bring with you when you move in and live there. As you see, calculating the weight of the *live load* can get a little tricky. Not only do you have to calculate the weight of the people and the things, you also have to know where they will be in the house, and you have to allow for rearranging the furniture and such.

Not to worry, we design professionals have simplified all of this and assume a uniform *live load* on every square foot of the house. Typical *minimum* uniform *live loads* in a house would be 30 pounds per square foot (PSF) in the bedrooms, 40 PSF and up in the living areas, and 20 PSF on the roofs. Just to give you a comparison, the minimum *live load* in a parking garage for cars is usually 50 PSF. Minimum uniform PSF *live loads* are dictated by the local building codes that have jurisdiction over the construction of the house. I emphasize the word *minimum*. Some builders and design professionals assume that the code-required minimum is all you need to think about. It meets code, right? You probably will want more than the minimum in certain rooms of the house, especially if you have a large family and everyone hangs out in the kitchen for family dinners, or you like parties where there are a bunch of drunk men singing some college fight song in tune with the cheerleaders on the TV while watching their favorite football team, and set the room in harmonic motion with its natural frequency and bounce everything to every which a way. That's when the word *assume* takes on the meaning of making an "ass" out of "u" and "me." I am very careful in selecting the *live loads* that I will use on a house, and I always select them after I have talked with the owner or builder about exactly what is going to go on in the house.

Wind loads are just that. The faster the wind blows, the higher the load or force on the house. *Wind loads* can get tricky too. If you have an odd shaped house or certain shaped roofs, the wind can cause suction and uplift on a house. If the house is taller than it is wide, the wind can be the governing load on the foundations and try to tip the house over. This would put uplift loads on the foundations. Large covered porches can also create areas for uplift. The roof of a house can create uplift forces if it is too flat. This is somewhat like an airplane wing changing the wind pressures. Uplift forces would require the foundations to be larger than normal to add weight to counterbalance the uplift, or they may require deep foundations, such as piles. *Wind loads* are in the range of 20 PSF for a wind speed of ninety miles per hour and are typically not a problem for most houses. However, if your house is on the ocean or a large body of water or on the top of a mountain, or in a city where the wind can be funneled between two buildings into a narrow opening, or anywhere where the wind can blow a five-pound rooster into a one-gallon wine bottle, the wind will have to be seriously addressed and designed for in the structure and the foundations. Houses located in hurricane-prone areas should be designed for the hurricane wind loads up to around 150 miles per hour. Tornado winds are so high (200 miles per hour and up) that the codes do not require designing for them. You *can* design for them, but think bunker-type underground structures.

Seismic or earthquake loads should be addressed in areas where damaging seismic activity is known to happen. Seismic activity happens everywhere all the time. It's just so small that humans cannot feel it and it causes no damage. In places like Japan and California, it's a big deal. Over the last thirty years, the engineering profession has spent a great deal of time studying earthquake loads and how to design for them. Believe it or not, we can mathematically model a structure, apply a seismic event, get resulting forces, and say we designed it for an earthquake. Everyone sleeps nicely at night until the next big one happens, and then it's back to the drawing board. In reality, the earthquake forces are so high that we cannot economically design for them; therefore, we divide them by an R factor to get them in line with wind loads. Also, although we say we design for earthquakes, the codes only hope that the building will not fall down and the people can get out. In earthquake areas, if the magnitude of the earthquake prescribed by the codes actually hits, it is a given that the structure will be destroyed, but, hopefully it will not collapse.

Basically, to keep it simple, per code, you move the house horizontally (in reality in any direction) very quickly and stop it, and the mass of the house keeps moving, creating a force. This force after the R factor would be in the range of 20 percent of the weight of the house. As you can see, the heavier the house, the more the seismic force. Most houses are built out of wood and are much lighter than other structures; therefore, code-required seismic forces in houses are almost negligible. Seismic forces for houses are usually much lower than wind forces, and most codes do not require houses to be designed for earthquakes. One- and two-story structures usually have very low seismic forces unless they are very long or very heavy. Usually when the house is designed for the *wind loads*, it will more than meet any requirements for *seismic loads*, even in California. Just to keep me in good graces with the seismic engineers, there are many good things that have come out of the seismic studies over the last thirty years. Most of the information has been incorporated into the building codes, such as requiring steel reinforcing in masonry work. Nevertheless, as an old engineer once told me, "When the big one comes, all bets are off."

Roof loads are a type of *live load*, but I want to expound on it anyway. The roofs have to be designed for a minimum of 20 PSF. If you live in areas where there is snow or ice, it usually has to be designed for more than 20 PSF. You may think snow doesn't weigh much, but consider this: You have a nice clean snow, and everything is pretty and white in the morning. The sun comes out and melts or thaws the snow somewhat, turning it into slush. Then it freezes again at night, and it snows again, and the same thing happens for several days in a row. Now you have a buildup of ice, of which four inches will weight 20 PSF. The shape of roofs also can cause buildups of snow or ice. A high roof that dumps its snow on a lower roof can really overload the lower roof. Roofs that have blind valleys (a terrible thing for a house to have) or that are flat should be avoided. If you are building in an area with snow or ice, be sure your roof knows it.

I think now you have a handle on the types of loads the foundations have to carry. But just to recap, *dead and live loads* usually act downward, due to gravity. *Wind loads* act horizontal, up, and down. *Seismic loads* are assumed to act horizontal, but your guess is as good as mine on that. One last thing on loads: they usually are either concentrated, such as the load under an individual column or pier, or they act uniformly down a line, such as a load under a brick wall.

The earth that the house is built on I will call the soil. If you have cleared your house site and are ready for the foundations and the soil looks like it would be good to plant a garden in, you probably have not stripped off the topsoil yet. This topsoil is called organic material, and you should never build on it. After you have stripped the topsoil (usually no more than twelve inches), you usually find that the soil is sand or clay or a combination of these called "sandyclay" or "clayiesand," depending on which is dominant in the mixture. This soil will be either virgin soil or fill material. Most sites will be virgin soil—but not always. There are cases of developers developing a property where some areas were not suitable for houses, and in order to sell them, they filled the areas with fill material to make the area more attractive for a house site. Another example of a fill area is in a remote area like a track of farmland. Over the years, the farmer had used a piece of his property as a garbage dump, and everything from old refrigerators to the dirt dug out of his pond was used to fill in this area. As the years passed, this area was leveled out and became overgrown like the surrounding property. The farmer died, and his relatives did not know about the fill area and sold the property to be used for house sites. Some people enjoy finding rusty old refrigerators in the backyard while they are planting a tree, but not me. These people probably will call an archeologist thinking they have stumbled upon the remains of an ancient civilization that had refrigerators.

Virgin soil is soil that has never been disturbed, and if it is strong enough, it is much preferable to fill material. Fill material, also called fill soil, is material that is used to change the elevation of your site. All houses will use a little fill material, such as final grading for the garage floor or patios built on the ground. When the fill material gets more than twelve inches thick, that's when you need to be extremely careful. If your house is going to be built on fill material, I strongly recommend that you hire a structural engineer and a geotechnical engineer to assist you in the foundation design and construction. Fill material must be put in under controlled conditions and compacted properly to avoid very large settlements. Even if you place fill material properly, it will usually give you more settlements than virgin soil. Also, the thicker the layer of fill material, the larger the settlement. It is not advisable to build your house half on fill material and half on virgin soil because they don't consolidate at the same rate and the potential for differential settlements is greatly increased. If you must build on fill material, hire the engineers, and minimize any potential for movement.

All soil that is suitable to build on has what is called an *allowable soil bearing capacity*. This soil bearing capacity is usually in the range of 2,000 pounds per square foot and up. Try to envision taking a one square foot of steel and setting it on the ground and stacking weight on it until it starts to sink into the ground. Once you have that weight, you divide it by a factor of safety, usually around 3, and that is your design soil bearing capacity. That's really not the way they do it, but it will give you an idea of what soil bearing is all about. If you left the weight on the steel for around five years, the plate would probably sink more into the ground due to consolidation of the soil. Loose soil, like loose sand, will consolidate more than dense, firm sand. Soft clay will consolidate more than hard clay. Fill soil will consolidate more than virgin soil. If your soil is 2,000 PSF soil, and you put more than that plus the factor of safety on it, the soil will fail and the steel will punch into the ground. The bearing capacity for most soils is well known and usually not a concern for most houses.

What is a concern, and something I have seen on more than one occasion, is differential settlements. Differential settlements usually occur not because the foundations were under-designed but because they were not proportioned properly. Let's say you add up all the loads for a certain foundation system. You take the heaviest load and design all the foundations for that load. The foundations with the lighter load would certainly not be under-designed, for they would be the same size as used for the heaviest load. However, if you maxed out the 2,000 PSF bearing on the heavy foundation, the lighter ones would only use say 1,000 PSF. Consolidation is directly related to the amount of weight a specific area of soil is holding up. So if one square foot of soil is holding up 2,000 pounds and the one adjacent to it is holding up 1,000 pounds, the one with the heavier weight will consolidate more. You want your foundations to be proportioned so that they are all using approximately the same bearing capacity. A column with a heavier load should have a foundation bigger than a column with a lighter load so that they consolidate at the same rate.

Thankfully, the loads and forces in average houses are so small that differential settlements are so small they are not noticed; but in the case where there are large differences, they should be accounted for. If you are building your house in an area that has a high water table, say within a few feet of the ground surface, you are probably near a body of water and you will need to account for that in the foundation design. Water tables fluctuate with rainfall, and water makes soil lose some of its bearing capacity. Also, if you dig a hole for a foundation, and it fills up with groundwater, you will need to pump it out while you are building your foundations. Once again, water must be addressed when building a house. Most houses are not built in areas where the water table is high enough to be a concern, such as a swamp—but if it is, be careful.

Types of Foundations

There are many different terms to describe the types of foundation systems used in house construction. I am going to touch on three types and describe them with my terms, although they will be called different names in different areas.

First is the *slab on grade system*. This type of system is probably the most simple, and in areas of the country where the frost line is a few inches below ground surface and the water table is not a concern, it is used a lot. This system consists of pouring a concrete slab on a prepared ground bed. This concrete slab on grade is the sub floor of the house. Any type of finish floor can be attached to the sub floor. This ground bed should be a little higher than the surrounding ground so that the rain will run away from the house. Also, this ground bed should be strong enough to support the house.

Around the perimeter of the concrete slab, the edge is deepened to around sixteen inches with a bottom twelve inches wide to form a toe footing. Areas in the interior of the slab that will be supporting wall or column loads are thickened to around twelve inches deep and twenty-four inches wide or larger. Steel reinforcement should be placed in the toe footings and in the thickened slab areas, and a wire mesh should be placed in the slab areas. The concrete in this entire system is usually placed in one continuous pour. Some people say that you do not need the wire mesh in the slab areas. I say you do because all concrete cracks over time. The steel wire in the concrete slab holds the concrete together and does not let the crack open up or grow. Also, the steel wire adds tensile strength to the concrete, which it will need for volume changes due to temperature and shrinkage. If you ever get the chance to jackhammer concrete with wire and concrete without wire, you will find out very quickly why the concrete with wire is better. However, over the centuries, there have been many, many, many concrete slabs poured without wire mesh, and they are still around today. Wire mesh is very inexpensive compared to the other parts of the house, and I think it is well worth the cost. If you are going to use wire mesh, get it in sheets, not rolls. The rolls are much more difficult to get and keep flat, and when you're rolling it out, if you unroll it the wrong way, it will fly back on you with those pointy wire tips. A modification to this system would be when you have short perimeter walls on the exterior instead of toe footings. The way that works is you build a perimeter wall, usually with a wall footing and a masonry or concrete wall, and back fill with compacted fill material to the height of the perimeter wall. A concrete slab on grade with thickened areas is then placed on the fill material. As the perimeter walls get higher than two feet, it is usually more economical and better to use another foundation system.

The second type is a *pier and wall* system. This system consists of a grid of individual masonry or concrete piers or columns built on their own individual foundations. The top of these piers should be at least two feet above the ground surface. The area between the top of the piers and the ground surface is called the *crawl space*. I prefer the crawl space to be high enough so you don't have to crawl on your belly if you have to go in there to retrieve some meowing kittens that the mother cat decided needed to be born there or to check on something. Most codes require that these piers do not exceed eight feet on center under the load-bearing parts of the framing of the house. These piers should be designed to carry the loads that are tributary to them and spaced accordingly.

Sometimes masonry or concrete walls will be used instead of a row of piers. Sometimes walls are used instead of piers around interior rooms, such as a den with a dropped floor or the garage. Around the exterior perimeter of the house, there is usually a masonry wall between the piers or taking the place of the piers. This perimeter wall may be load bearing or not. When it is not load bearing, it is usually called a *skirt wall* and can be made with most any suitable material; it is used only to enclose the crawl space of the house to keep wind and animals out. Other times, it is used to carry loads; and if it is, the perimeter walls should be designed for those loads. If a perimeter wall is used, it should have openings in it to ventilate the crawl space and to help keep it dry. It is desirable to have two access doors on opposite sides of the house.

The third type is the *basement or cellar* system. This system consists of exterior perimeter walls usually of masonry or concrete that are below ground surface and form rooms that are high enough to stand up in. The water table in these systems should be well below the bottom of the foundations, and even then sometimes water or moisture has a way of getting in. The framing of the house is supported on the perimeter walls and interior load-bearing columns or walls. This basement may be entirely underground on all sides or have only one side underground. It will depend on the type of site the house is on. These basement walls will need to be strong enough to resist the backfill and house loads and will have to be waterproof. Concrete is much more preferable than masonry for these walls because masonry has inherently more joints to let moisture through even if it is laid up solid.

The way this works is a hole is dug usually several feet wider than the basement. Wall foundations are placed, and the exterior basement walls are built. The basement concrete slab on grade floor is then placed. This slab may have thickened areas for column or wall loads. Next, the framing of the house is installed to provide weight on the exterior walls and to brace them. The exterior walls are then waterproofed and backfilled. It is always wise to put some type of protective sheeting between the backfill material and the waterproofing to keep the backfill material from damaging the waterproofing while the backfill is being dumped in. If the exterior walls are backfilled prior to framing the house, they must be designed to resist the backfill loads without being braced; it is much simpler to brace them with the house framing, but sometimes it is not possible to do that. Some people, including me, recommend that the basement floors that are entirely enclosed by four walls be slightly sloped to a central point so that if water were to enter the basement, it would run to that point and could be pumped out with a sump pump system. If the basement is not entirely enclosed, the floor should be sloped to an open side just in case that water thing happens.

There are other types of foundations for houses, but these three make up the largest part. Some houses use all three of these systems in the same house, and some don't use any of them at all, such as a house on piles.

Houses with piles or deep foundations are non-typical types of houses. These types of foundations will require a subsurface investigation and a structural engineer. Pile foundations are either wood, the most common for houses, steel, concrete, or composite (plastic). They are installed using cranes equipped with pile-driving attachments. They can be driven, drilled, or vibrated into place or sometimes a combination of those three depending on the soil conditions. Once they are installed to the proper depth, they are cut off at the required elevations, and the framing of the house is attached to them. If they are cut off at ground level, usually a concrete cap is placed on top of them and then the foundations for the house. Pile foundations are out of the scope of this book, but to give you an idea of how they work, they are just like giant tent pegs. If you install them right, you don't have to worry about them. If you do not, they will be a great big pain. Piles can be reused—that is, if they are installed at the wrong location, they can be pulled out and driven again. Piles are driven to refusal or until they are deep enough to develop the forces on them through skin friction and end bearing with the surrounding soil. Once piles reach refusal (you keep pounding on them, and they do not go any further into the soil), you must stop driving them or the top of the pile will start to splatter with each hammer blow. Piles can develop up or down and sideways forces. Up forces would put the pile in tension, and you have to be careful with tension piles. It's like pulling out a tent peg; once you get it a little, they come out easily.

Cassions are like piles only bigger. They are drilled into the ground to the proper depth and filled with concrete and rebar. They usually have to be big enough for a man to go down in and check the bottom or sides. Cassions are usually lined so that the sides of the hole do not cave in while they are being drilled. After they are drilled to the proper depth, they are filled with concrete and rebar, and then the casing is pulled out. If you need piles or cassions, you probably have a high water table and that will have to be addressed also. As you can see, you will need some engineering if your house needs deep foundations.

There are other types of foundations you could use for a house, but they are variations on those mentioned above. What you need to remember about your foundations is this: do not skimp on them and get them right the first time. In most areas, the building official requires that the excavations for the foundations be inspected prior to the placement of the concrete. They usually check that the soil is in good condition and the rebar is installed properly. The contractor should have grade stakes or elevations marks on the sides of the excavation to be sure the concrete is poured to the right level. If your foundations go in level, square, plumb, and with the right dimensions, the rest of the house will be level, square, plumb, and with the right dimensions. If the foundations are not put in right somewhere during the framing of the house, all of that will have to be corrected with some goofy type of work that will look very odd. If it is not corrected, the walls will not be straight or plumb and the corners will be out of square and things like that. If the contractor tells you it's all right and that you won't be able to see it because it will be covered up with the finishes, get ready for all types of excuses for the shoddy work that's going to come. A good contractor knows that if the foundation is right, it makes the rest of the framing and finishes easy. Be sure to check out the contractor or the subcontractor who's actually doing the foundation work prior to digging the foundations. An experienced, conscientious, foundation contractor should have plenty of references and be happy to talk with you about his fascination and experience with concrete.

I cannot emphasize enough the importance of a sound foundation. Although its time in the bright sunshine is very short, take some pictures of this stoic mass of concrete and masonry and hope to never see it again—because if you do, something has gone terribly wrong. Modifying a foundation with the structure already resting on it is an expensive nightmare. So, be sure everybody involved with your house is aware of your love and passion for the cold concrete. It is the one part of your house that should never let you down even though it should require no maintenance and you should never see it again when it is finished.

Chapter 3
Masonry and Fireplaces

Masonry fireplace with stone facing

Masonry

Once the concrete foundations are in place, the foundations' walls or piers will be next, and they are usually made of masonry. Traditionally masonry consists of stonework, brickwork, clay tile work, CMU work (Concrete Masonry Unit), and any material that is laid up with mortar. The standard unit for masonry work is four inches and multiples of four inches. Although there are many different sizes of brick, the standard is one brick is four inches wide and eight inches long, and three bricks stacked up with mortar joints is eight inches tall. Again, there are many different sizes of CMU types, but the standard CMU is eight inches high, sixteen inches long, and the width varies between four, six, eight, ten, twelve, and sixteen inches. The most common are four, eight, and twelve inches wide. Foundation walls with several feet of soil backfill should be at least eight inches wide. Foundation walls with no backfill are commonly known as *curtain walls*, and they are usually four inches of brick and a maximum height of forty-eight inches. These types of walls usually require piers every eight feet, especially if they get higher than forty-eight inches. Building codes have height to thickness ratios for walls that are not designed by a licensed engineer. This ratio is usually the height is no more than twelve times the width; an eight-inch wall would be ninety-six inches tall (eight feet).

If your house does not have a basement or is not a concrete slab on grade then it will have a crawl space. This is the distance between the top of the foundations and the bottom of the framing. Most codes set this distance as twenty-four inches minimum, and they say that if the wood is at least twenty-four inches above the dirt, it does not have to be treated. So most crawl spaces are at least twenty-four inches high. There is a considerable amount of stuff that can go in a crawl space, such as plumbing, HVAC, and sometimes storage. All of this stuff will have to be accessed at some point, so as I mentioned earlier, I recommend that the crawl space be as high as possible to allow people to get around in it without actually crawling on their belly.

Also, if possible there should be access into the crawl space on all sides of the house. Most houses only have one access door, and it's usually far away from whatever you're going into the crawl space to get. Anyway, the walls and piers around and in the crawl space most likely will be brick and CMU, hopefully solid or grouted solid. The height of the crawl space, whatever it is, should be in increments of eight inches to work masonry.

If it is not that dimension, then the mason will have to cut the units to fit the height; this is called hogging. It is not pretty, and it requires more work than if the foundation is placed at the proper elevation to allow for full height units to be used without cutting. A good contractor is going to set the distance between the top of the foundation and the bottom of the framing in increments of eight inches.

There will be piers in the crawl space. These are usually made sixteen inches square with two eight-inch CMU block. Remember, CMU blocks are eight inches tall and sixteen inches long, and using two that are eight inches wide makes a sixteen-inch square pier. These piers should be located eight feet on center under the main stringers in the house, but most builders put them eight feet on center in both directions, and then add them wherever they have a concentrated load coming down. The eight feet on center is usually a good spacing for the strength of wood, but if the space is fourteen feet long then, rather than eight feet and six feet, it would be better to use two spaced seven feet. It's all just common sense. Putting a little thought into the layout and height of the crawl space is all it takes to save a lot of aggravation.

Masonry work can be laid with solid units or hollow units. If the work is with hollow units, it's usually grouted solid with a fluid grout. If you do not grout the hollow units full, it becomes a pest condo. Grouting the cells full also helps prevent the masons from putting their lunch trash into the hollow parts of the blocks. I highly recommend that all masonry work below the framing be solid or grouted solid.

If your house has a basement or a portion of the ground floor set into the earth, the walls will be in contact with the soil. In this case, reinforced concrete is the best material for the walls. If you want the brick or stone finish, you can cast a masonry ledge near the top of the concrete walls, and the parts of the wall that are above ground level can have a brick or stone skin and have the look you want. Some builders prefer to use CMU to build these types of walls. They start with an eight-inch CMU and at the top change to a four-inch brick and a four-inch CMU. Of course, if the wall is tall, they would have to start with a twelve-inch CMU and then change to a four-inch brick or stone and an eight-inch CMU. However you do it, the walls will have to be reinforced with reinforcing bars to handle the loads from the soil that's backfilled up against them. Unless the walls are concrete, the CMU cells with the rebar will have to be filled with grout.

Some builders fill only the cells of the block with rebar in them. They do not fill the whole wall solid. This is not a good idea. If you have these types of walls, the mason should fill all the joints solid with mortar and fill all the cells with grout. The mason should take extra care with the basement walls to be sure there are no voids, or eventually water will find that tiny crack and then moisture problems begin. Even concrete walls will develop hairline cracks and the same moisture problems can occur. I think you can see there are many more joints in masonry work compared to the solid concrete walls. Either way you go, the basement wall underground needs to be waterproofed. There are several companies that make waterproofing membranes for basement walls. These membranes should be applied per the manufacturer's recommendations. I recommend that after the waterproofing is applied, a protective layer of black board or some type of non-organic sheeting be put over the waterproofing to protect it from the backfill operation. Most builders backfill with a crushed rock like #57 stone to allow drainage, but this rock can scrape or scar or penetrate the waterproofing as it's dumped in from a loader. All of this is to let you know that you do not want water in the basement.

Some people like brick or stone for the exterior skin of the house. This exterior skin is usually four inches thick, and due to the height to width ratio, the wall can only be forty-eight inches tall. Since the exterior masonry will be much taller than forty-eight inches, it will need to be connected to something that will keep it from rolling over. Think of stacking up bricks until they just fall over. What that means is that the skinny wall will fall over if it's not attached to something strong enough to hold it in place. In this case, the masonry skin must be attached to something else to brace it laterally. This something else could be another course of masonry to make the masonry width thicker or to the wood framing. Either way, the masonry skin is attached to the supports with masonry ties. Masonry ties are simply metal pieces that attach to the wood and stick into the joints in the masonry. They should be spaced around sixteen inches on center, both horizontal and vertical. If the wall is eight inch CMU and four inches of brick, there would be a strip of ties at sixteen inches on center vertically. Remember, three bricks equal eight inches vertically, so that works the eight-inch block backup.

No matter what type of material the masonry is, it is bonded together with mortar. Mortar is usually a mixture of sand and Portland cement and lime. Sometimes mixtures are added to the mortar to color it or enhance some of its properties, such as stickiness, time to set, and the like. There are usually three types of mortar used in residential construction. They are called Type M, N, and S. Type M is the best; it has the most Portland cement in the mixture, which makes it more durable, and it's used for all masonry underground. Type N is used for masonry that will not be exposed to the exterior elements; therefore, it is only used indoors. Type S is used for exterior work not in contact with the ground.

The joints that the mortar goes into are called head and bed joints. The bed joints are horizontal, and the vertical joints are called head joints. Both of these joints should be completely full of mortar from front to back of the masonry unit. The width of these joints should be three-eighths of an inch wide. The mortar is put into these joints a little thicker than the three-eighths of an inch and then mashed down and sideways to the desired thickness until the mortar squishes out of the joint. The joint is then struck off with the trowel so that you have a straight flush joint. Masonry work is usually laid up around four feet high and then allowed to set up. If you go much higher than that, the joints tend to mash with their own weight and become out of plumb or level.

Once the mortar is set up, the joints are tooled to the desired profile. This tooling is important because it seals the outer surface of the joint and makes it more waterproof. The most common joint type is the concave shape where a round, steel tool about three-quarters of an inch in diameter is pulled and pushed over the joints to give it the concave shape. This also seals any voids between the masonry unit and the mortar. There are several different shaped tools to dress out the joints. There are V joints, bevel joints, fancy shaped joints, and the list can include any type of joint you want to make in the mortar. The key is to make sure the joints are tooled in some way to seal it as tightly as possible. Usually at the end of the workday after the mortar has set, the wall is brushed off with a stiff brush to clean any masonry off the surface of the brick. If you do not brush off the masonry, it becomes difficult to remove from the brick and looks cruddy. Some masonry work is cleaned with high-pressure water after it has set for a few days. This really cleans all the mortar from the masonry and leaves the wall with a good finished look. Sometimes contractors clean the masonry with a muriatic acid wash, but you have to be really careful with this because it can change the color of some masonry. The essence of all of this is to leave the masonry work with pretty, tight joints without leaving mortar all over the wall.

Fireplaces

Cooking oven and fireplace made of concrete

Fireplaces are usually made of masonry. However, today you can get fireplaces made of metal and other non-burning composites. These fireplaces work fine and are approved with the proper fire ratings. They even have ceramic logs that use gas to burn and look just like real wood-burning fireplaces. Since some of these fireplaces do not have chimneys, they work like a gas stove. I guess I'm just set in my ways, but I like the old masonry wood-burning fireplaces that you can throw things in to burn like yesterday's newspaper. You can't do that with ceramic logs. If you use ceramic logs, you do not want to clean out the ashes. Whatever you like, you use. I just like the custom of building a fire and smashing a cognac glass against the masonry firebox if you get romantic like that. In this book I will only be discussing masonry fireplaces; if you want a different kind, you can look at them at the fireplace shops or online. Masonry fireplaces are just that—they're made of masonry from stone to cement bricks, and they have a chimney, sometimes with a neat chimney pot.

Fireplaces can consist of some or all of the following: ash pit with clean outs, an air intake vent, firebox (this is what you see when you think of a fireplace), hearth, throat, damper, smoke chamber with smoke shelf, flue lined chimney, sometimes fancy trim work and a mantel, and sometimes doors or screens. The design of all these items is important, but the most important thing is to design the fireplace so that it does not smoke and draws properly. The proper relationship between the size and height of the chimney flues and the height, width, and depth of the firebox is all it takes to ensure you do not have the misfortune of a smoking fireplace. There are many different equations and rules of thumb for the proportions of these dimensions.

A couple of these rules of thumbs are that the cross-sectional area of the flues should be one-eighth to one-twelfth the area of the fireplace opening, and the depth of the firebox should be a minimum of half the height. The one-eighth to one-twelfth the area for the fireplace opening is dependent on the height of the chimney above the hearth: one-eighth for twenty feet, one-tenth for twenty to thirty feet, and one-twelfth for more than thirty feet. Use the next larger flue size if the flue area to opening area is short. I advise, for fire protection, to encase the flue with a minimum of eight inches of masonry an all sides. If you have more than one flue, then a minimum of four inches between flues is all right.

When building a chimney, great care should be taken to ensure that the joints in the brickwork and the joints between the brickwork and flues are completely filled with mortar to eliminate fire hazards. The insides of the flue should be as smooth as possible with no rough mortar projections; they should also be as straight as possible. The shape of the firebox should be such that the heat will be thrown out of the box and not just go up the chimney. This requires the back and sides to be sloped toward the front opening and form the throat of the firebox where the damper is located. The throat leads to the smoke chamber with the smoke shelf and then to the chimney. The designs of these parts of the fireplace are important to ensure that it works properly. I think the best way to guarantee there will be no problems with the fireplace is to hire an experienced mason who will guarantee that the fireplace will work, and test it before you pay him.

The working parts of the fireplace are dictated by the required ratios for a successful smoke-free job. The other parts are there for aesthetics and comfort. I like a hearth that is sixteen inches off the floor so I can sit on it while making a fire or cleaning out the ashes. Some hearths are flush with the floor; that makes it hard on my knees. No matter where the hearth is, it must be made with a material that will not burn. The codes require the hearth to be a certain size in front of the fireplace for fire protection. For that matter, the codes have other requirements for the fireplace, so be sure to check the codes with regard to your fireplace construction. Some people like the face of the fireplace to have fancy trim work and a mantle. I think all fireplaces should have a mantle, and the amount of trim work is up to your specific tastes. The damper in the fireplace usually is controlled by reaching your hand inside the top front of the firebox and adjusting the handle of the damper to open or shut it. I like a damper that has a handle sticking through the face of the fireplace so you don't have to reach inside the firebox to adjust it. Also, the handle of the damper won't get the black soot on it if it's outside the fireplace.

Having an ash dump is a really good timesaver and makes cleaning the fireplace easier—if the clean out for the ash dump is easily accessible. Having an air intake vent allows the fireplace to burn without sucking the heated air out of the house. It works by having a vent from the outside of the house leading into the firebox for combustible air. If the fireplace is located too far from the exterior wall, this may not be practical, but usually it's a good idea.

I think fireplaces have been around since humans learned how to build a fire. They're an essential part of a house if you ask me, but otherwise unnecessary. If you want a fireplace, spend a little time studying it to be sure it will be a pleasure and not a hassle.

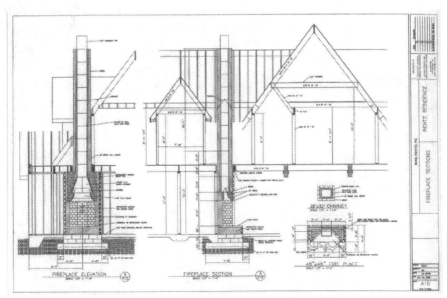

Figure 3. Typical fireplace drawing

Arches and Corbels

Simple brick arch

Arches, patterns, and corbels add to the distinctive appearance of quality masonry work. Arches, if built right, are one of my favorite types of architectural jewels that you can incorporate into a house. There are all types of arches, from flat to round and Arabic. Arches in masonry are made by two methods. One is to cut the masonry units into wedges, and the other is to use wedge shaped mortar joints. Cutting the masonry units into wedges looks the best, and I think it's the proper way to build arches; however, it's more labor intensive and slower than just using wide mortar joints. There are some masonry suppliers that have premade arch units that are somewhat expensive but really dress out an arch. Arches are built with a formwork that is removed after the mortar has cured. The flatter the arch, the more thrust it has on each support, and a perfectly flat arch should have a steel lintel carrying it. A perfectly round arch has no thrust on the supports. When building an arch, the supports must be able to resist the thrust; this is necessary for strength and appearance. An arch setting on small, narrow supports looks like it might push the support sideways; and if it looks like it will do that, it probably will over time. One way to build an arch is to lay the pieces out on the floor so that you can see how they interlock and then build the support and lay the pieces up on it. If you are going to use arches, spend the time making sure they will be pretty and strong.

Corbelling brickwork adds depth and shadows to the wall. It also adds ledges for water intrusion. When corbelling, the unit should only stick out a maximum of one-third of its depth. For a four-inch brick, that would be 1¼ inches. Some masons set corbels on top of corbels to create large reveals. Be sure to lock the reveals back into the wall to prevent weak areas. This is usually accomplished by turning the brick long ways into the wall and using the four-inch side on the exposed face. Turning the brick to use all of its faces creates the designs in the brickwork that makes it so distinctive. Of course, the creative design has to make sense and not create ledges that can potentially hold water. Make sure the corbelled ledges have a slight slope for positive drainage away from the wall.

Some of the best masonry work in the world can be found at the University of Wisconsin, Madison. It's amazing what true skilled masons can build with bricks. It's also amazing how ugly poor masonry work can be. It has always made me wonder when I hear the Historical Architectural Preservation Society types talk about the value in preserving old brick warehouses simply because they're old.

The masonry work in most of these building is very poor. This includes the mortar, brick, and workmanship. In the old days before steel wire reinforcement, when a multiwythe wall was built, every two to four feet a course was turned perpendicular to the wall to tie the wythes together. That and some pilasters every so often in the walls are all the reinforcement these masonry buildings have. By today's codes, they are grossly deficient. Except to be used as an example of how not to build with masonry, I can find nothing in these building that warrants saving. It always costs more to retrofit these buildings than to tear them down and build new ones in their place. These building are mostly two- and three-story, old warehouses that were built along the railroad tracks. They were used simply to keep the water off the goods.

Most of today's warehouses are the least expensive, prefabricated metal skin buildings that you can construct. All they're supposed to do is keep the rain off the goods, so spend the money on the corporate headquarters and not the warehouses. It makes sense now and made sense then. I find it ridiculous when I hear uninformed historical society types cry about losing our heritage when it's even suggested that one of these dilapidated warehouses be torn down. If the masonry work has the following, you have a historical mess that should not be considered sacred: powdering mortar that is turning to sand; flaking, crumbling bricks; mortar joints that were never laid full and are way too wide and out of level; walls that are not straight and plumb; no maintenance for decades; unreinforced masonry that's structurally unsound.

There are masonry structures that are indeed works of art that were made by true craftsmen and deserve being treated like a monument, but most warehouses were built to be a warehouse and are well past their time. Whatever you do, make sure the masonry work in your new house does not look like the work in these old buildings. Make sure your walls are straight and plumb. You can do this with your eyes just by sighting down the edge of the walls. Make sure the joints are the same size and are tooled, and the brick is brushed clean of mortar. Be sure that the people doing the brick or stonework are true, experienced masons that take pride in their work.

Even the best masonry work has some inherent issues that sometimes create problems with the finished work. The first is that, all masonry, especially brickwork, absorbs moisture, especially when a driving rain blows horizontally against the walls. Most brickwork on houses has an air gap between the brick and the sheeting on the house. The sheeting on the house behind the brickwork should be damp-proofed. This is accomplished by coating the sheeting with a waterproofing membrane or wrapping the house with plastic. The air gap between the waterproofing and the brick allows any moisture to be pulled down by gravity into the gap, hopefully before it gets to the house.

The second issue is efflorescence. These are the white stains that sometimes appear on the face of masonry after it's been exposed to moisture. It's the dissolving of salts like sodium, lime, and magnesium found in the masonry and mortar and depositing them on the surface of the wall. It's the result of moisture in the wall. It's prevented by using material with low salt content and proper flashing and caulking. However, I think all masonry walls, especially brickwork, will show some of this eventually. Efflorescence usually is not an indication that the material or workmanship is defective, and it can be cleaned off, but that's not a cure.

Masonry work is one of the oldest types of construction. It offers a great variety of choices in color, surfaces, patterns, jointing, style, and more for both the interior and exterior of the house. If built properly, it is one of the most maintenance-free exteriors you can use on a house and therefore one of the best.

Brick house with concrete slab on grade foundation

Chapter 4

Framing

First-floor framing for a beach house right on the ocean. This house has survived hurricanes Hazel and Hugo. Note there is no metal strapping as required by modern codes.

The rough framing of the house is my favorite part of the construction of a house. You always have a fellow in the framing crew named Alvin, or something like that, who had his nose bit off by his cousin during a family fight. He works as a carpenter only during the winter when he's not hunting; the rest of the time he makes moonshine or farms or something else. Alvin usually isn't the foreman of the framing crew, and he'll probably get fired sometime during the construction of the house for something like urinating off the roof during the bank's monthly inspections, barely missing the bank's inspector. Alvin will think that's really funny, and the other members of the crew will too—until Alvin gets fired. My friend said that her dad always told her she would step on a nail if she wasn't careful, so she couldn't go watch the work in progress; I think it was because he didn't want her to meet Alvin.

I think you can tell the quality of the framing crew by the type of sawhorses they use and their ability to nail 20-penny nails with three licks, and most importantly by the music they listen to, the jokes they tell, and how early in the job Alvin got fired. Alvin usually won't get fired until the really dangerous work like framing the roof ridge is done—that is, unless he has a really bad day. There's always one member of the crew that's the master carpenter; he could be named Tony or something like that. He's usually the oldest and says he can figure his taxes with his framing square, or so he claims. Most likely, he won't know trigonometry, but he has an amazing way of working out double bevel cuts in wood circular stairs and the other hard cuts involved with house framing.

Then there's Timmy the toe nailer. He's the fastest nailer until he hits himself with his hammer and gets a bleeder. Alvin will usually have something comforting to say to Timmy when that happens, such as, "If you don't stick in it your mouth, you'll turn into a woman." Then he'll try to get some of the guys to tie him up so he can't. Tony will usually know a comeback to Alvin's jokes, such as, "The head on those nails is on the wrong end," and then Tony will say, "Those nails are for the other side of the house." The framers are a very motley crew, and I highly recommend getting to know them all.

While there are very good framers who have considerable knowledge about the tried and true methods and materials used in house building, their knowledge tends to be handed down from the old timers. "That's the way we always did it" is the reason for doing it again. While there's much to be said for "if it isn't broke, don't fix it," having a structurally sound, well thought out framing plan is simply a must. A little planning goes a long way.

Let's begin with the material, wood or sawn lumber. There are many different species of wood, and they each have their own properties. The species most used in house framing are pine, fir, and redwood. It depends on which part of the country you're building in. Pine is the most common in America. Sawn lumber comes in many different sizes. Everybody knows what a two-by-four is, but not everyone knows that a two-by-four is actually one and one half by three and one half inches. Sawed lumber is called by the nominal dimensions even though the actual dimension is different. The length of lumber usually ranges from eight feet to twenty-four feet in two-foot increments. If you need six-foot lumber, you will probably be buying twelve-foot lumber and cutting it in half. If you want a thirteen-foot two-by-four, you'll have to buy a fourteen-foot piece. A twenty-six-foot piece would be a special order if you can get it at all. Don't get me wrong, you can get it—trees grow bigger than twenty-four feet—but the wood industry is set up a certain way, and if you deviate from the standards, it gets very expensive. It's always best to order lumber in the length you need and minimize the cuts. Cutting lumber means unloading the lumber at the work area, loading it on sawhorses, measuring and marking it, cutting it, moving the lumber to the area to be nailed up, then cleaning up the saw area. If you cut it wrong, you do it all again. Cutting it wrong usually doesn't happen. There's an old saying that all good carpenters know well: *measure twice, cut once.*

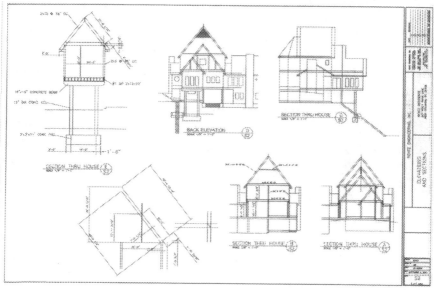

Figure 4. Plan showing the geometry involved with the framing of a house

Most houses will use a wood product called plywood or a derivative of plywood made from wood chips and glue. This plywood usually comes in four feet by eight feet sheets and thickness from thin veneers to three quarters of an inch and up. You can special order plywood to most any thickness and length, but again, if you get away from the standards, it's very expensive, so the four feet by eight feet module is standard in house framing. Use four feet by eight feet for plywood, or if you want, four feet by four feet. Remember four feet modules along with the knowledge that lumber comes in two-foot increments starting at eight feet. Careful planning can save a lot of cutting and prevent wasting material.

For example, let's say you wanted a shed in your backyard to store your Christmas decorations and old milk cartons. You thought fifteen feet by fifteen feet would be big enough. You would have to buy sixteen-foot lumber and cut it, and you would have to do the same with the plywood. You would have to pick up the ends you cut off and haul them off. With some thought, you could go to sixteen feet by sixteen feet, have no cuts with associated labor and clean up, and have a bigger shed that cost less. Remember, you had to buy the sixteen feet of lumber anyway, and it costs more to cut and then nail rather than just nail, so your labor would be less. This is a very simplistic way to explain framing, but think of applying this to a whole house. Just the cleanup of the ends alone is worth a little thought and planning. Check the dimension of your house plans to be sure they work with lumber dimensions. I always wonder about the designer that has a dimension like 13'-9 11/16" rather than 14'. Sometimes this is unavoidable, but most of the time it's not, and it pays to work this out on paper before you begin framing. If your house plans are full of dimensions that do not work with lumber, find another designer.

The quality of the lumber needs to be considered. Lumber comes in grades, such as #1, #2, #3 select structural, and many other types of grades. This grade relates to its strength, straightness, and the number and size of the knots in the piece. Something like #1 select clear would be the best with no knots, and #3 would be warped and full of big, ugly knots. Most lumber dealers will tell you #2 lumber is okay for house construction. They would be correct in that it usually is structurally strong enough, and it's the one most commonly used. However, I have found that #1 lumber is just as economical as #2 and you get a better product. There are always pieces in #2 lumber that have to be discarded because they are really #3. Number 1 lumber can usually be used all up. The labor to nail a #1 piece is just the same as to nail a #2 piece. So the only cost difference is the lumber, and I think, when you have to take out the pieces you shouldn't use from the #2 lumber, you might as well have bought #1 and saved the labor to sort it out.

Most good carpenters will not use ugly lumber anyway because Alvin or someone like him likes only pretty lumber—especially pretty, pretty,

pretty lumber—and he could get in a bad mood messing with warped knotty boards. I personally think that's because it never fails that the knot is always right where you need to drive the nail, and it's extremely difficult, if not impossible, to drive a nail in a knot even with a nail gun. So now you have Alvin with a bleeder, and it never fails that the bank inspector is on the way. You get the idea; working with nice pretty lumber is more fun than fighting ugly, warped knotty lumber, and the end product says quality.

One thing about lumber that most people don't realize is that it moves. If you took a nice, pretty, straight two-by-four, laid it on two sawhorses, and left it there for a few months, it would move with the direction of gravity and would no longer be straight. If it was not completely cured when you set it on the sawhorses, it would warp and sag down. That's why the floors in old houses are usually out of level. It's not because they were made like that; it's because lumber moves with time and gravity. This phenomenon is called *creep*. Lumber and concrete do it, but steel does not. If you bought lumber in an area with a moist climate and took the lumber to a desert, it would dry out some and shrink in length and width. Lumber will acclimate itself to the ambient moisture content of the area it is used in. It can shrink or expand depending on the moisture content.

If the moisture content goes over 19 percent, then it will rot. You want your lumber to be off the ground and dry, and you do not want water to get on it. Lumber that you use outdoors, such as for decks, should be treated, and that will help it last longer when it's exposed to the elements. By "last longer," I mean ten to twenty years, depending on the type and amount of treatment you use to preserve it. When using lumber for your decks, turn the grain of the lumber down so the boards cup downward. If you don't do this, the board will cup up and hold water. Look at the end of a board to determine which way the cup is turned. Also, in areas where termites are severe, such as South Georgia, or areas where there's high humidity and high moisture contents in the ground, framing your house entirely with treated lumber, even the plywood, is a good way to stop termites.

The first floor of the house, unless the house is a concrete slab on grade, is the beginning of the framing process. The first floor is built upon the piers and foundation walls. Most codes today require that lumber that comes in contact with masonry or concrete be treated lumber, or there needs to be a metal or plastic barrier between the masonry and wood. I personally don't think it does any good because I've seen many houses and wood structures that were built without this requirement and are perfectly fine. The treatment leaches out over time anyway.

Most codes require the wood framing be at least two feet above ground or the wood must be treated. I highly recommend that the distance from the lumber to the ground be at least two feet and preferably four feet. It's almost impossible to go into a crawl space that's only two feet high, especially if you have to work in that area to fix a leak or change a filter or something like that. Whatever the crawl space height is, the space should be well ventilated. Proper ventilation is necessary to keep this area dry, and the dryer the better. The local codes will tell you how big and how often the vents need to be. These vents are inexpensive, so use a few extra and buy a good quality closable vent. There should be an access door to the crawl space. It is much better to have two access doors, one on either side of the house. It never fails that the cat had her kittens as far away from the access door as possible, and if you're crawling on your stomach, even a short distance is too long, especially if the ground isn't dry.

Once after Hurricane Hugo came ashore on the Isle of Palms, South Carolina, I was asked to inspect a house with a two-foot crawl space. This house was on the highest part of the island and one of the only houses that had not had the water rise above the first floor during the hurricane. I was barely a few feet into the crawl space when I saw the snakes. The owner was amused and told me that the other inspectors had seen them too. He apologized, but said that he knew if he told me, I would not go in. Needless to say, I did not find it funny at all, and although I had heard that they had really good grits at the local jail, I thought it best not to find out firsthand. I wished him luck and a few other things as I drove off.

If your house has a basement, forget everything I just told you about crawl spaces, except at the perimeter wall keep the dirt two feet below the wood.

Floors

Wood floor systems can consist of many different types of framing. There is the standard two-by-four lumber, and there are wood floor trusses, wood I beams, LVL, glulam, and so on. If there are long spans, such as over garages or great rooms, there will probably be steel beams involved. All these systems have a subfloor attached that's usually plywood, and all these systems have two important areas that need to be addressed. First, it must be strong enough to hold up all the loads that will be applied, and second, it needs to hold these loads up without movements (deflections) that can be perceived by human beings or movements that would distress finishes attached to them or sensitive equipment supported by them.

Most codes have a minimum deflection that's allowed for a certain floor, wall, or roof system. These deflections are defined by the span or length of the floor member divided by an empirical number like 360 that over time has been found to work. This number 360 has been found not to crack sheetrock ceilings. There is no scientific basis for these numbers, just experience. I have found that when the floor spans exceed fourteen feet, most codes' deflection criterion is inadequate, and people will feel the movement. For example, a code-required deflection of L/360 for live loads at twelve feet would be twelve feet times twelve inches per foot divided by 360 (12 x 12 / 360 = .4 inches = 3/8"). You probably would not feel three-eighths of an inch. An eighteen-foot span would be .6 inches (18 x 12 / 360 = .6"). A twenty-four-foot span would be .8 inches. Most people will feel that very easily, but it is allowed by code.

When I design a floor system for a residence, I like to make them stiffer than the code requires by closing up the spacing of the floor members or making the floor members bigger. When you have a floor system that will have a finish floor of ceramic tile or something brittle, the systems need to have a minimum deflection of L/600 or larger, no matter what the span is, or the tile will crack with the movement. If there's going to be sensitive stereo equipment or the like, the floor will need to meet the stiffness requirement of the equipment. Any competent structural engineer can tell you what your deflections would be for the floor system, and you can decide if you want them stiffer.

The stiffer the floor system, the less likely it is to squeak. Squeaking noises come from members rubbing against each other. If the floor does not move, the members will not slide against each other. If the members are attached properly, they should not move, but making it stiffer helps. Movements in structures are not bad or wrong or against the codes. Most people have felt floors move in office buildings, parking garages, and structures like that. When we drive a car, it moves all over the place, but we're used to the movement and it doesn't bother us. If you can determine the natural frequency of a structure and apply a force at that frequency, you can collapse any structure. This is like making a car bounce by pushing on it with the right timing, especially if the car has bad shocks. Nevertheless, when it comes to people's home, they simply do not like to feel it move, and I don't either. So be sure your floors are stiff enough. The time to do that is with the designer, not after you walk on it.

Walls

The walls of your house are either interior or exterior walls. Some people also say they are load-bearing or non-load-bearing walls. All walls carry some load, even if it's just its own weight. I have found that "non-load-bearing" walls somehow pick up some load along the way, so be careful with them. All exterior walls are most definitely load bearing. They carry everything they are supporting, and they also have wind blowing on them. They usually provide most of the lateral stability for the framing. This lateral stability is provided by the plywood or wood type sheeting on the walls or X-bracing in the walls. The amount of the sheeting or X-bracing needed on the exterior walls will be determined by the geometry of the house and the wind speed and seismic forces that could come into play. Usually, if you sheet the entire exterior of the house with plywood, that will provide the necessary lateral stability for the house.

If your house has a lot of windows and not much wall space or is a unique type of geometry, such as taller than it is wide, you may need to sheet some interior walls as well or use other types of bracing, such as metal straps. Some people will tell you that you do not need to sheet the entire exterior of the house, to just sheet the corners and fill in the rest with another type of material. They may be right on some smaller houses, but I think it's better to sheet the entire exterior, and I highly recommend it. There is something about black board or sheetrock or Styrofoam that just doesn't seem strong enough to me for the exterior walls. Some people say you get better insulation values with material other than plywood. I will get to the insulation a little later.

Two other characteristics of walls are the height and thickness. The taller the wall is, the thicker it needs to be. Most walls are in the eight to nine feet tall range and are made of two-by-fours, called wall studs, sixteen inches on center. These are the usual types of interior and exterior walls for one- and two-story houses. If your house is more than two stories, the first floor will need to be double studs or go to two-by-sixes, sixteen inches on center. As the house gets taller, the walls must get stronger accordingly. Most houses over three stories are out of the range of typical residential framing and will involve more of a commercial framing system, such as steel or concrete and the use of cranes and the like.

Walls also must accommodate utilities like plumbing and electric lines that are installed in them. A two-by-four wall with a three-inch plumbing line running horizontal will obviously not work, and the wall will need to be made with wider studs. All walls need to allow for the meat of the wall being drilled out to run utility lines. These walls are usually around bathrooms, laundry rooms, and near main electrical breaker boxes. Some walls will need to be made wider simply because they are carrying more weight from built-in cabinets or a heavy sculpture or concentrated loads from the house. The exterior walls will be sheeted and have some type of exterior finish applied to them. These exterior walls usually need to be stronger than the interior walls simply because of the wind loads they have to carry along with the gravity, live, and dead loads.

The exterior finish will be something like brick, cement stucco, synthetic stucco, wood lumber, plastic or vinyl boards, cement boards, stone, and it goes on. All of these finishes have their own way of attaching to the exterior wall, and they all attach easier and better if the exterior wall is sheeted with plywood. I highly recommend that all the exterior walls be made of two-by-six wall studs sixteen inches on center. The main reason for this is to allow for five and a half inches of insulation in the wall cavity. Also, once you drill for the utility lines, you usually take away one inch of the thickness, thereby making a two-by-four really a two-by-three (1½ x 2½) and a two-by-six a two-by-five (1½ x 4½). There is very little difference in labor between a two-by-four and a two-by-six wall. The material costs are higher, but the extra insulation more than offsets this cost over the life of the house with savings in the heating and cooling bills.

Thicker walls allow less movement in the exterior and interior finishes that are attached to these walls. Less movement means the walls are less likely to crack or open up at the joints of the finishes during high winds or seismic events. I do not recommend two-by-six walls for the interior of the house unless the wall needs to be thicker for utility lines, sound insulation, strength, looks, or to accommodate built-in items in the walls. Hidden doors and secret compartments are always fun to do with walls; they're easy, and the framing crew loves them. Walls that are supporting ceramic tile, such as in bathrooms, kitchens, and laundry rooms, would be better if they were treated lumber just in case you had a leak that was not found for years.

Just to repeat this, for one- and two-story houses, the walls are usually two-by-fours at sixteen inches on center. If the ceilings are around nine feet tall and there aren't many holes drilled into the studs for wires and pipes, this is usually strong enough. If the ceilings are twelve feet tall or the walls are near electrical main boxes or main large plumbing lines, the walls' studs will be full of holes and the walls will need to go to two-by-six or larger. If the house has three stories, the ground floor walls will need to be two-by-six at sixteen inches on center or double two-by-fours at sixteen inches on center. As you can see, as the house increases in stories, the lower floor walls need to increase in size. If your house is four stories, you will most likely need a structural engineer to design the framing.

As all good carpenters know, it is very important for the walls to be built plumb, level, straight, and square with each other. This makes everything that attaches to the walls, including finishes, trim, cabinets, mirrors, pictures, and whatever else easier to install. It also makes the wall look right. If the wall is not straight, it will show up with a bow in it, especially if something straight like cabinets or shelves are attached to it. The same is true for plumbness of the wall. If the wall is leaning in, the pictures will not be flat against the wall and the doors won't work right. If the corners aren't square, the trim will look goofy. It just makes sense to get the walls right at the start and keep them right with temporary braces, rather than having to fight the walls for the life of the house.

Roofs

The roof and attic framing of a house needs careful consideration. The appearance of the house is greatly affected by the rooflines, and the functional use of the attic should never be neglected. Roofs can take on many different looks. There are round, dome roofs, onion shaped domes like in Russia, flat, single slope, shed type roofs, hip roofs like a pyramid shape, and gable roofs. There are combinations of some of these types. The most common in residential construction is the gable and hip roofs and the combination of both of these. Consider a simple square or rectangular house. The gable roof starts at the eave in the front and slopes up to the ridge and then back down to the eave. On either end of this type of roof is the gable, which usually has big vents at the top for airflow. The hip roof starts at the eave on each side, slopes up, and comes to a point if the house is square or a ridge if the house is rectangular. Shed roofs are usually a single slope and start at the face of an exterior wall and then slope down to the eave. Houses that are not square or rectangular will have roofs that intersect each other and create valleys between the ridges. Valleys collect more of the water on a roof than any other area. They need careful consideration, and the roofing material needs to be installed correctly.

All of these roofs will be constructed with some type of rafters and roof sheeting that will support the waterproof roofing material.

The rafters involved in the roof framing will need to be sized to carry the live and dead loads that will be supported by them. The dead loads would be the type of roof covering: red clay tile, slate, asphalt shingles, wood cedar shakes, copper or other metal sheets, rubber membrane, thatched weeds, and so on. The live loads would be wind, snow, ice, seismic forces, and people or anything that can come and go on the roof like satellite disks or even helicopters. Depending on where you are, the snow or wind loads can get heavy. The minimum live load a roof should be designed for is twenty pounds per square foot. This is about four inches of snowy ice. Most competent contractors experienced in the areas they are building in will know the span, spacing, and size the rafters need to be.

I do not recommend that rafter spacing exceed twenty-four inches on center and recommend sixteen inches on center. One thing to keep in mind about rafters is that most roofs are asphalt shingles, and after thirty years or so, the shingles will need to be replaced. Some roofers like to just nail new shingles right over the existing ones; this doubles the weight of the roofing material, and that should be considered. I don't recommend doing that. Take the old shingles off. That allows a good inspection of the roof sheeting for any damaged areas, and then you can add the new ones. Once the rafter spacing has been determined, the roof sheeting will need to be selected. The roof sheeting needs to be thick enough so that it does not sag between the rafters; this just looks really bad. So, the further apart the rafters are, the thicker the roof sheeting needs to be. Also, the thickness of the roof sheeting will be determined by how the roofing material is attached to the sheeting.

Certain roofing material requires longer screws or nails than others, and some people do not like to see the points of the nails coming through the roof sheeting. Most roofs with asphalt shingles in the southeast United States are two-by-six rafters at sixteen inches on center with half-inch plywood nailed six inches on center with 8cc nails. There is very little snow in the southeast. If the snow loads increase, the rafter size will too. All rafters need to be supported at the appropriate span length by the load-bearing walls in the house. The configuration of the bracing for the rafters will determine how efficiently the attic space can be used. Since very few people walk or spend much time on the roofs, the movement of the roof is never seen or felt and is allowed to deflect much more than a floor system would. Thus the strength of the roof system is more important than deflection.

Some houses use a roof truss system for the roof and attic framing. While this is a very economical system, the web members of the roof truss tend to eliminate the use of the attic for any type of efficient storage area and also make it difficult to get around in the attic if the need arises. This is especially important if the HVAC systems are located in the attic. If you need to get around in the attic to change filters or work on the heating or cooling systems in a house, the attic space for the HVAC systems should be easily accessible.

The slope of the roof should be determined so that the house has the appearance the owner wants. However, the slope of the roof will affect other areas of the house, and these areas need to be considered. First, flat roofs leak, and you always need to have some positive drainage to the eave, so never use a perfectly flat roof. Slightly sloping roofs can have a ponding effect if they're not sloped enough to exceed the deflection of the roof rafters. For example, you have a flat roof, water gets on it, and it sags some due to the weight of the water and makes a little pond on the roof. More sag, more water, more sag, and it can go on until it collapses. That is the ponding effect. A roof should slope enough so that ponding cannot occur. Usually a minimum slope of one inch in eight feet will be enough to prevent ponding. It's very difficult to walk or work on a roof that's sloped more than a 7:12 pitch. This means the roof rises seven inches vertically for every twelve inches horizontal. A 7:12 pitch creates approximately a thirty-degree angle with the attic floor. A 12:12 pitch creates a forty-five-degree angle and so on. To get a feel for this, most stairs are around a 7:12 pitch; lay a board on the stairs and try to walk up. Now sprinkle some sawdust on the board and try to walk up. That's why carpenters knock the sawdust off the plywood before they hand it up to the roof. The steeper the roof, the more difficult it is to build and install the roofing material.

The slope of the roof also affects the live loads that it supports. The building codes say that roofs sloping less than around a 6:12 will have uplift forces from the wind. Depending on how fast the wind blows, these uplift forces can become very large and require hurricane clips on the roof rafters and metal tie downs extending to the foundations. Even roof slopes exceeding 6:12 will create uplift on the leeward side of the ridge according to the building codes. What this means is that if you're building in a high wind speed area, low-pitched roofs will fly away if you don't tie the roof down really well. These uplift forces or suction tend to suck the shingles off the roof unless they're attached well or are heavy like tile or slate. That's probably why a lot of the houses in Florida have red clay tile roofs. Those red clay tiles last longer in the sun than asphalt shingles.

In heavy snow areas, low slope roofs tend to build up larger amounts of snow. Steep roofs let the snow slide off easier. You have to be careful not to let a steep roof shed its snow load on a lower level roof, especially if that roof cannot shed its snow. The recommended minimum slope for asphalt shingles so they won't leak is 4:12. Headroom in the attic also must be considered. A house with a single gable 4:12 pitch (the roof sloped from the front eave to the ridge and then to the back eave) would have to be thirty-six feet wide to just have six feet of headroom at the ridge in the attic. As you go from the ridge to the eave, you have to bend over, and this is not fun, especially if you're working on a HVAC system and the attic storage space is minimal. The same roof with a 7:12 pitch would have ten feet of headroom at the ridge. For most houses, I recommend considering a minimum of 6:12 pitch and going up from there.

The main function of the roof is to keep nature's elements, such as sun and especially water, out of the inside of the house. The steeper the roof, the faster water runs off. Sometimes a roof can be so large and so steep and designed so poorly that the water volume becomes a problem. An example would be a large roof area that directs the water to a valley, creating a large volume of water running very fast that shoots right over the gutters. This is a terrible problem because the roof is built and does not work right. The roof on a house is supposed to shed the water off the roof as efficiently as possible. This means running straight down the roof to the eave or a gutter. Every time the water has to change directions to get to the eave, there is more potential for leaks. Having water run into blind valleys or dead valleys is a big, big, big no-no. The roof will leak; it's just a matter of time. A blind or dead valley is an area of the roof that does not drain efficiently, if at all. It usually forces the water to turn ninety degrees and build up some in order to flow off the roof. These types of valleys collect leaves and other types of debris that inhibit the flow of the water even more. They require maintenance to keep clean; I have seen a small tree growing in the debris collected in a blind valley. One thing to keep in mind about leaks in roofs: When the water penetrates the roofing material, unless it's a big hole like a tree branch falling through the roof, the hole is small and the water is in dripping amounts. This water will run down the underside of the roof sheeting for some distance before it drops off onto the attic floor or house ceiling. The location of the leak in the ceiling is usually downstream from where the leak is in the roofing material.

Rooflines are what give the roof and house some of its appeal, or if done wrong, make it ugly. The combination of hips and valleys and sheds and domes and turrets and the like needs to be worked out so that the roof functions properly. Although some roofs look like they were cut with pinking shears and have all types of ridgelines and valleys, to me these roofs are just too complex to be pretty. They usually require more maintenance, and there's more potential for leaks. Roofs that are made of slate or clay tile are usually clean and simple with minimal ridges and valleys. It's most likely this way because the material does not lend itself easily to ridges and valleys the way asphalt shingles do. Ridges should be as far apart as possible. I have seen houses with layers of hips and ridges barely far enough apart to be able to roof properly. Perhaps the designer or owner wanted the roof to look this way, which is fine with me, but these roofs are difficult to build and difficult to maintain and are ugly. Layers of hips can be eliminated by making the roof slopes steeper; it makes the house look bigger and is less expensive to build. With a little thought, most complex, chopped up roofs can be transformed into a clean, elegant, simple roof with majestic, high ridgelines. This will give you an efficient roof with plenty of space in the attic.

House roof with blind valleys and weird lines. This roof just looks odd. Roofs should be clean and simple.

Attics

To me, the attic space has always been one of the most interesting places in the house. If it's built right, it will provide plenty of storage space for the old trunks the kids like to go through and all of the kids' old junk you just can't throw away. I have seen attics that were just an afterthought to the roof framing. The bracing of the roof rafters was so goofy that it was difficult to get around without running into them, and they were installed at weird angles such that you had to duck under them. I have also seen attics with plenty of headroom, but there was minimum floor sheeting, so you had to walk on the ceiling joist and there was nowhere to store anything. I have seen attics where the ceiling joists or attic floor was not strong enough to support anything in the attic, although there was plenty of room for it. That's such a waste. If your roof is not steep enough for there to be headroom in the attic, it should be. Make sure you frame the attic so that it can be used as an attic is supposed to be used, and make sure there's easy access to it.

Access to the attic can be from a door off an upper floor or with pull-down stairs. If you use the pull-down stairs, get the oversized commercial grade to make getting to the attic easy. Everywhere there is headroom should be sheeted for a floor, and the floor designed for attic storage. If the HVAC systems are located in the attic, there should be plenty of space around the systems and easy access to them so that maintenance is simple. If your roof is framed with trusses, try to use the type of truss (like a fink type truss) that allows you to have attic storage. Always take advantage of the attic space. It seems like almost free space to me.

The next two pages contain drawings showing attic framing, floor plans, and elevations. These are typical house plans. Having a visual representation of the material I have been discussing will help you start to put things together in your mind and may help you when you begin designing your own house plans.

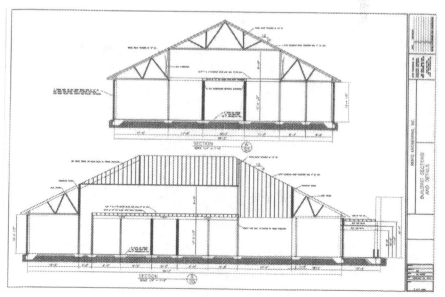

Figure 5. Plans showing attic framing

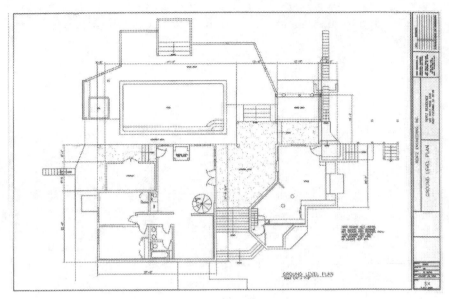

Figure 6. Ground-floor plan

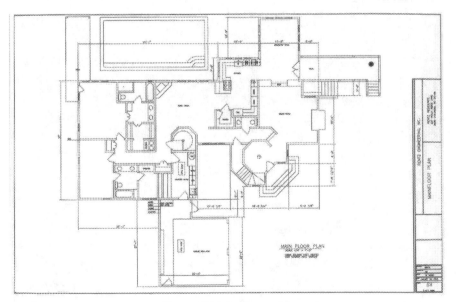

Figure 7. Main-floor plan

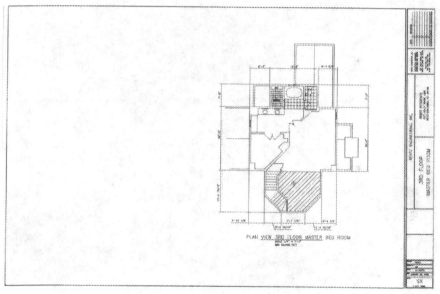

Figure 8. Third-floor plan

Chapter 5

Roofing

This house has a clean, simple gable roof.

As we have seen, there are many types of material that can be used for the roofing of a house. The roof framing must support the weight of this roofing material and all the forces that will act on it. The roofing materials' main purpose is to keep Mother Nature's elements off the interior of the house and its contents and people. Simply stated, the roofing keeps the rain off us—along with the snow, wind, sun, dust, and whatever else can fall from the sky or be blown by the wind. The next purpose of the roofing material is to look pretty and function maintenance free for as long as possible.

In order for the roofing to do its main job as easily as possible, the rooflines need to be as clean and simple as possible. This way, the water gets off the roof as fast as possible. This water should flow to the eaves and then down and away from the house. Or it should flow into gutters around the eaves of the roof, then to downspouts and onto splash blocks on the ground, and then away from the house. It does no good for the water to funnel into downspouts and then empty directly onto the ground beside the exterior wall of the house. I know this sounds like a good way to water the shrubs around the house, but the water will dig a hole and saturate the soil in that area. The soil will turn to mud around the foundations and make the house settle.

The best splash blocks are made of concrete or clay and come in all shapes and sizes. Many splash blocks are plastic. Some are architectural jewels and add a distinctive feature to the house. The gutter needs to be large enough to handle the amount of water that will flow to it; if not, the gutter will fill up and overflow.

Downspouts need to be spaced so that the gutters do not have long runs to get to them. The gutters have to slope to the downspouts; so if the downspouts are too far apart, the gutters will look odd because they're sloping and the eave line is straight. In areas where water is scarce, the downspouts can direct the water through pipes to holding tanks or cisterns to be used later. This water usually has to be purified in order to drink it. All gutters need to be cleaned out over time, even those with leaf guards on them. I guess you could say that's one reason for not having gutters, but I highly recommend them if they are installed correctly and are going to be cleaned out properly.

Interior gutters are usually associated with low sloping or flat roofs. I highly recommend that you do not use them unless there is no other way. These gutters are usually formed by a parapet or short wall at the eave of the building that rises above the roofing and the roofing material itself. The drains for these types of gutters are located a few feet inside of the eave with the roofing material sloping toward it. The parapet acts as a dam to force the water to the drains and then to downspouts that are located on the interior of the house. Usually in the parapet wall (and around four inches above the roofing material) a scupper is located adjacent to the drain. This is so when the drain clogs up, the water can only build up four inches on the roof. Needless to say, if the drain clogs up, the scupper probably will too. Now you have a lake on the roof and guaranteed leaks. Also, if the interior downspout fails, then you discharge water into the interior of your house. Do not use interior gutters unless there's no other way to accomplish the look of the roof you want—and then don't use them anyway. Then, the roofing can do its main job and not leak on your head while you're showing your house to your in-laws.

Selecting the roofing material and color is one of the main decisions the homeowner makes. Light-color roofs reflect light and thus heat; dark roofs do the opposite. Sunlight bakes the roofing and is the main cause for a roof wearing out, becoming brittle, breaking, and needing replacing. Roofing material warranties vary with the type of roofing. Clay and slate last the longest, wood shingles the shortest. Asphalt or fiberglass shingles are the most common, and some claim to last thirty years. Metal roofs, steel, aluminum, and copper last a long time if the right thickness is used. Steel roofs will have to be galvanized and/or painted. There are many types of asphalt or fiberglass shingles that have architectural textures that give the roof some degree of depth and look like wood shakes or slate. The cost of roofing should be looked at with a life cycle perspective.

The clay or slate roof material and labor will cost more initially, but it should be a one-time expense during the life of your house. Wood shingles would be one of the least costly, but there would be considerable maintenance with them over the life of your house. Asphalt shingle roofs offer the best value for the money.

I recommend a 7:12 pitch with clay tile if you live in an area where it's sunny most of the time and it fits the style of house you're building. Otherwise, for the rest of the country, a good quality asphalt or fiberglass shingle will do just fine and also offer you more of a selection of colors and textures. As the owner of the house, be sure you pick a roof color that you like. Changing the color is a little more difficult than painting a wall. Look at other finished roofs to be sure you have the right color and style.

Ventilation of the attic space under the roofing material is very important. As the sun bakes the roofing on the outside, heat builds up on the inside of the attic. This heat needs to be minimized by the use of louvers, eave and ridge vents, and exhaust fans. I was in one attic with no vents, and the heat was 90°F on the outside and 145°F on the inside. You could only stay in the attic for a few minutes, and the roof had considerable problems. There are many types of vents, but the two most common are ridge vents and eave vents. These are premade and match the roofing material used. Ridge vents run along the top of horizontal ridges and let the air out at the very top of the roof, which is usually where the hottest air is. The eave vents are usually in the wood trim directly under the eave of the house. Eave and ridge vents work together to let air flow in from the eave and up and out through the ridge. Gable vents or louvers are usually installed in the gable ends of roofs at the highest point. These types of louvers are premade and come in various sizes depending on how much ventilation you need. All of these vents should have screen wire and hardware cloth to keep bugs and critters out of the attic.

Exhaust fans usually penetrate the roofing near the highest points in the roof framing. They need flashing around the edges. These fans have a thermostat located in the attic. When the heat in the attic reaches a certain predetermined range, the fan comes on and sucks out the hot air through the fan while sucking in cooler air through eave or gable vents. Exhaust fans are used when no other type of vents are practical and should be avoided if possible. Exhaust fans require maintenance, while vents and louvers do not. All ventilation systems need to be installed properly and per the manufacturer's written recommendations. I have seen ridge vents installed directly over the shingles, which closed the vent. I have seen attic insulation placed over the eave vents, which closed them too. Be sure the vents are installed so they function as designed. The use of properly sized gable, eave, and ridge vents will keep the attic temperature in acceptable ranges and help prolong the life of the shingles used in the roofing.

All roofs have nasty little things called penetrations. These penetrations are the result of plumbing vents, chimneys, electrical conduits, exhaust fans, and anything that needs to penetrate the roof or be mounted on it. They are all potential leaks and must be flashed properly. Plumbing vents are the most common, and they come with a premade sleeve that fits around the vent pipe and under the shingles or roofing. I would make sure the builder uses the highest quality sleeve available. The location of these penetrations can take away from the look of the roof. Be sure they are located somewhere out of sight on the roof and are as close to the color of the roof as possible. A white pipe penetrating a black roof will stand out, especially if it's right over the front door.

The installation of the roofing material and flashing must be done correctly. Insist on using only roofers that have experience in the type of roofing you select, and make sure they have been in business for at least ten years. Select a roofing company that operates in the area where your house is being built and check that company's reputation. Do not use a roofer who's moonlighting away from a company or someone who's a jack-of-all-trades including roofing. Roofing is a specialty trade, and the roofing material must be installed right for looks. All good roofers know that leaks make people mad. All roofing manufacturers want their product installed the correct way and with the correct amount of fasteners. Always be sure the roofing is installed per the roofing manufacturer's written recommendations or your warranty on the material will be void. If you feel the roofing is not installed correctly, ask a representative of the roofing manufacturer to inspect your roof. They usually will not charge for this. Even a good roofer will tell you all roofs will leak sooner or later. He is probably correct; however, a good roofer does not want it to leak in his lifetime, so be sure you get the best roofer you can.

One small note, a good roofer will have a magnet that he will use to pick up roofing nails, staples, or fasteners that roll off the roof during installation. If he does not have one, be sure he picks the nails up by hand. Roofing nails are short and have a big head. They always tend to land with the point up and can make even your grandmother say a curse word.

House with a complex floor plan, and although part of the roof is steep, it is a simple gable roof.

Chapter 6

Windows and Exterior Doors

Triple windows and double doors

Doors and windows, especially doors, will be one of the most used features in your house. They are therefore one of the most important. There are many types of doors and windows, and they come in many sizes, styles, and materials. Since we are dealing with residential construction, we will stick mostly with these types of doors and windows. Most home-supply business and specialty shops will have the various manufacturers' products in stock and on display in their stores. In these stores, you can get a feel for the products and their prices. You will find that doors and windows can be from simple and economical to complex and expensive. Before you pick out these products, let's talk about what they really are.

The Basics

When you think of doors or windows, think about them as being a box that you place in the wall. That box can be any size or shape you want. The more boxes you put in, the more it costs. Inside of the box, you could have one door or window, or two or three or four or however many you want. If you have a wall where you want a lot of glass, you could install four boxes with one window in each, or you could install one box with four windows in it. What's the difference? I'll explain.

Each box has to be laid out in the wall in its own opening, and then it has to be framed around with side jambs and jack studs and bottom seals and top headers. Then each box has to have its window or door installed. This involves shimming, leveling, plumbing, attaching, and waterproofing the window or door to the wall opening. Then the exterior skin has to be fitted around each box. Next, the interior of the window has to be dressed around with the wood trim. Again this involves the sides and bottom. Then you have to paint or coat each box. Then the window or door hardware and the blinds or drapes have to be installed. So as you can see, the more boxes, the more the cost. If you want three windows in a wall, consider a three-unit window in one box. There would be less work all around. However, some people want the look of a thin sliver of wall between each window for aesthetic reasons; if that's your cup of tea, sip it up.

To keep it simple, think of boxes when you're thinking about your windows and doors because what goes in those boxes can get complex, which means expensive. If the tops of your doors or windows have to have arches, you are out of the box theory and the cost of your windows or doors just doubled. Don't get me wrong, I think some doors and windows in certain styles are worth the extra time and cost, and the wall and house sometimes just feels better with an arch here and there in it. I especially like a french paired arch casement window that opens out with no screens. By french, I mean no jamb between the window; this gives you a big open area where the birds can fly in. One drawback to this window is that it's hard to seal the two windows without a jamb to latch them to in the middle. I guess you have to take the good with the bad, so start with the boxes and go from there.

Doors

Double dutch doors are cool and practical

Doors are usually divided into two categories, interior and exterior. Exterior doors are usually larger and thicker than interior doors, and to me, their main function besides entering and exiting the house is security. Exterior doors are usually thicker (1¾"–2¼") than the interior doors (1⅜"–1¾"). Exterior doors are usually three feet wide, while interior doors vary in width but are usually two feet six inches wide. As people get older, they may need to consider doors that a wheelchair or electric scooter can maneuver through. This width will usually be three feet wide or more. Some exterior doors are double doors—two leafs that are two feet six inches wide for an overall width of five feet, which is plenty wide to get the furniture into the house. Interior doors need to be wide enough for that same reason. Bathroom doors tend to be narrower than other interior doors because most bathrooms will not need to have a grand piano moved into it. So the size of the door needs to accommodate whatever is going into the room the door leads into. The height of the doors is usually around six feet eight inches tall, with exterior doors being taller in some cases for looks.

Exterior doors, especially the main front door, create the first impression of the house when entering it. Garage doors are also exterior doors in the roll up or overhead category, and they also give that first impression. Dutch doors are really two doors, an upper and lower. I think they're really cool for back doors or shop doors. Pocket doors are mostly interior, and they have to be installed correctly because if they malfunction, you have to tear the walls up to fix them.

There are many types of doors made from many different materials. Exterior doors tend to be solid core, while interior doors could be hollow or solid core. Panel doors tend to be solid everywhere—that is, if they're made of wood. If they're made of fiberglass or Masonite, they may be hollow core. Metal and glass doors have their own styles and features. As you can see, we can go on and on about doors and their unique properties, so I am just going to say what I think about doors in a purely practical sense. Pick out the exterior front door you like that makes a statement about your house. Make sure it's at least three feet wide, six feet eight inches tall, one and three-quarters of an inch thick, and is made with a material that's strong enough (such as oak or mahogany wood, steel, or fiberglass) so that the door cannot be kicked in by a linebacker for the Green Bay Packers. If you have to have glass in the door, make the panes small enough so that a person cannot get through, or make the glass bulletproof.

The remaining exterior doors should match the function of the room they lead into. Use double french doors or patio doors if you have a patio, a soundproof door if you have a soundproof room, a lightproof door if you need lightproof, a lead-lined door if you have X-rays, but always be sure your doors are wide enough for the stuff in the room. If you're not careful, you can have too many doors. When two doors are close together, they're rarely both used; one tends to stay shut all the time. The location of the doors needs to be thought out. Say an interior door is two feet six inches wide and is in the middle of a wall. To open the door fully, you need five feet of wall. That's why most doors are placed near the corner of the walls, so the door will open against a wall and space is not wasted. Never have a door open where the light switch is on the side behind the door or the door covers a wall outlet or covers up the space for a good picture. I've seen that before, and it really aggravates the person trying to find the light switch. So be sure the door locations are worked out with the furniture, pictures, light switches, and wall outlets. This is easy to do upfront and prevents people from being called an idiot. Some doors have a window or transom over them to make them look pretty and let in light and ventilation, I guess. You can't look out of them, so I guess pretty is the main reason for them.

All doors have to be hung with hinges or pivots. Those great, big, beautiful solid oak doors are heavy and need oversized hinges or pivots, and even then, they'll work loose and have to be adjusted over time so they don't bang the jambs. When they close, they still can make a loud noise if closed too hard. There's something to be said for those lightweight, hollow core doors after all. One other thing about doors, those nifty little doorstops that fit on the hinges don't work unless you open the door very gently. If you swing the door open too hard, these rascals tend to spring the hinges; the door won't fit the opening anymore and scrape against the jamb. Use wall-mounted doorstops, and you won't spring the hinges, even if you're in a hurry.

All doors and windows need hardware. However, compared to the hardware available for doors, window hardware is boring. Basically, for windows, you just have hinges or slides, a handle to open them, and a lock to secure them. Doors, on the other hand, have all types of stuff: hinges or pivots, from the plain, old ordinary kind like the ones that would be on the crawl space door to the ball-bearing, self-closing, never need oiling, exotic metal, and grand-size ones like those on a castle door. There are doorknockers and doorbells, peepholes, and even little doors in doors to look out of. There are kick plates and push plates so the door will not be scratched by pets. There are many different types of doorknobs or latch sets with the same amount of keying arrangements. There are dead bolts, thumb bolts, slide bolts, and all sorts of ways to lock doors, both surface mounted and hidden within the door.

There are panic hardware and security hardware that will sound alarms or call the police if you want. There are self-closing devices and computer controlled hardware that will do most anything you want, from remote control to time clocks or motion or noise activated. As you can see, there is a lot to cull when considering door hardware. To simplify this, all doors need the minimum of hinges and a doorknob, and most will need some type of lock, even if it's simply the push button type. Visit your nearest door hardware specialty store or go online, and you'll be fascinated by the mechanical marvels available in door hardware. One other thing, do not be surprised at how much they charge for this stuff. A good quality keyed doorknob will start around fifty dollars, and then the sky is the limit.

Windows

Triple windows with a view

Windows also come in many shapes and styles. They are usually broken down into four types: double-hung (the most common), hinged or casement, pivoted, and sliding. I know of no restrictions, other than common sense, on the size of windows, except for windows in bedrooms. I understand most building codes require that at least one window in a bedroom must be able to be used for an exit, setting the size as at least 5.7 square feet with a minimum height of twenty-four inches and a minimum width of twenty inches. Building codes vary from region to region, so check with the local building official for clarification, or change the use of the room from bedroom to study if your window layout is so critical. I think this restriction is so that if you're sleeping in the bedroom and the rest of the house catches on fire, you can get out. If you're sleeping in the den, you're on your own if the windows aren't big enough or there are no windows at all. There are several quirks in the codes like that to try to protect us from ourselves. Another one is the height of stair steps, but that's another story.

The sash material the windows are made of is the same as doors. Glass for the windows has become very complex. Most windows use insulated glass—that is, two panes of glass with an inert gas or air or vacuum between them. Some windows use three panes of glass, some windows use bulletproof glass, and it goes on. Most of the heating or cooling loss that occurs in a house will be through the windows, so the better the window, the less heating or cooling loss you will have. I recommend that you buy the best windows you can for that reason. Also for that reason, I recommend that you minimize the number and size of the windows in your house. I know that everyone likes to sit and look out of the window at the beautiful sunset or to see the bald eagles flying or to see the sailboat coming over the horizon or to see the neighbors walking down the street and on and on. Unless your house has some majestic panoramic view from every room, I doubt you will be sitting and looking out the window for very long. Besides, most people cover up the windows with window treatments and look out only when they're opening the blinds, which they shut at night so no one can look in. Most people seldom open their windows. I always recommend screens on windows and think windows should be opened for fresh air and breezes as often as possible. Some people want windows for sunlight and that makes sense, although they usually turn on the overhead light too. After all that, most windows and their treatments are set in one position and seldom adjusted and seldom opened. Most people take a glance out of the windows every now and then. Even front doors without glass have a peephole if you want one.

The size of the windows needs to be determined. I think most people think bigger is better. If that were the case, then the exterior walls should be entirely of glass. I know that's stretching it, but think about the size of the window and the location of the furniture and pictures in the room. The top of the windows should be around the same height as the top of the doors, say six feet eight inches. Any higher and you couldn't see out of the windows without a stool, and they would be hard to get to for opening or cleaning. Most furniture is at least two feet six inches tall. The practical height of a window is around four feet tall beginning two feet six inches from the floor. I know it happens all the time, but why put a window in a wall and then cover up the bottom half of the window with a piece of furniture? Even if you have no furniture in front of the window, are you going to get on your hands and knees in order to look out the window? I have heard of people who like to lie on the floor for their back; perhaps they like to look out of the window then. If it works for them, it's fine with me. The width of the window should be considered also. Keep in mind that windows take away wall space for pictures and furniture. Some people like strip windows running completely across the wall from corner to corner. That's fine if there are no pictures, bookshelves, etc. The width of the window and the location of the window usually will work itself out after you have positioned the furniture in the room. I think two feet wide windows are plenty big; some people like them bigger. It's up to you and your likes.

I know this is seldom ever done, but the number and size of windows in a house should be kept to a minimum. This gives you more flexibility for the furniture and pictures in the room and minimizes heating and cooling loss. Daylight only comes in half of the time and you can only be in one room at a time, so the rest of the time, the windows are just messing with your hot or cold air. I'm not saying houses with a view shouldn't develop it, just get your lines of sight and design your windows and furniture to work with them.

I do not recommend skylights at all. They are penetrations through the roof, and the sun bakes them out. They are hard to clean, and unless kept clean, the light they were designed to bring into the room is filtered through dust and whatever else lands on the roof. Some people think they're neat; I think they're a maintenance problem.

While talking about windows, I always like to add this about mirrors. Some say they are the windows into the soul. For the money, you can't beat them. I think mirrors are one of the most interesting architectural features you can have. If used correctly, they are one of the most functional items in a house. On occasion, everyone likes to look at himself; most women find it an absolute necessity before leaving the house. Placing mirrors at strategic locations in the house will have interesting results. They always make the room look bigger. They reflect light, so the light from a window or light fixture will be enhanced. They are practical and somewhat mysterious, especially two mirrors that reflect into each other or change an angle down a hall or up a stairway. I have even seen them on ceilings, but there's something about glass over my head that seems dangerous. I guess I'm an old fuddy duddy that way. Have you ever seen someone that made you wonder if they even knew what mirrors were for? One-way see-through mirrors can be useful for those of you in the hidden room and secret door variety. Anyway, keep mirrors in sight while envisioning your new home in your mind's eye.

One more thing, if you're building in a hurricane area, the building codes are requiring a stronger glass than regular window glass or the use of functioning shutters. I never could understand why some people liked windows with fake shutters. I guess that's in the aesthetic area again where I tend to be underdeveloped. I think the stronger glass is good on the ground floor windows where someone could break in while everyone is evacuating from the hurricane, but if I were going to build near the ocean, I would definitely use shutters and all the other hurricane-proof ideas I could. Just keep in mind that when the big one comes, all bets are off.

Chapter 7
Exterior Siding

New cypress siding to match old cypress siding

The exterior finish of the house is the skin that will wrap the house from the roof eaves to the foundations. Traditional materials used for this skin include brick, stone, cement stucco, concrete, concrete block, wood, metal, fiberglass or synthetic material, cement or plastic boards, and new material like fabrics and Kevlar (think of tents). The three most common are brick or masonry, wood, and cement or synthetic stucco. All exterior finishes have their pros and cons.

All of these finishes attach to the framing of the house with some type of fastener. That's why I recommend that the exterior framing be sheeted with plywood or OSB type sheeting. Sheetrock, Styrofoam, black board, and other soft materials do not have the ability to develop the fasteners as wood does. Nor do they have the durability if they come in contact with moisture.

Consider the wind blowing on the house; the wind pushes or pulls the exterior skin into or away from the framing. Brick connections fastened through the soft material and into a stud will mash the soft material and allow more movement in the brick wall. While this movement may be small, masonry work does not like movement; it tends to make it crack. The same can be said for all exterior finishes: the more movement, the more room for cracking. So I like to attach the exterior material to as solid a surface as possible, thus plywood. One thing to keep in mind about plywood—it shrinks and swells like all wood, so it is recommended to keep gaps around the edges of the plywood to allow for this movement. Most carpenters will use an 8-penny nail to form the gaps as they install the plywood sheets. I have seen walls where the bottom sheet of plywood was installed and the next sheet set right on top of the first and so on up to the eave; and when it rained on the wall, it swelled up and buckled out away from the studs. The contractor had to come back and saw joints along the edges of the plywood to allow for the movement. The plywood associations provide recommendations with regard to gaps for the installation of their particular product. Most good carpenters know this already. So make sure your framing and sheeting are a good, sound backing for your exterior finish material.

Brick or masonry finishes on a house are heavy compared to other types of finishes like wood. Masonry walls have to set on foundations designed for them. It is very poor practice and against most codes to set brick or masonry on wood. The reason for this is wood moves a lot compared to masonry, and masonry just does not like a lot of movement, and it will tell you that with its cracks. Speaking of cracks, all masonry will crack sooner or later. The cracks may be so small you cannot see them, but they're there. Think of the nature of masonry; you have mortar made of one material and the masonry made of another. Mortar usually comes in three types: Type M for masonry in contact with the ground, Type S for exterior masonry, and Type N for interior masonry. Brick comes in all shapes and sizes; just pick the one you like and be sure it has a compressive strength of 5000 PSI. That's in the low range for brick, so most any brick will work.

Anyway, when you lay it up, you have many joints just waiting to crack with the slightest movement, even movement from temperature changes. For example, let's say you have a brick wall ten feet high and forty feet long. The temperature at night was 50°F degrees and during the day was 80°F. The coefficient for expansion for brick masonry is around .00034 for 100°F. All materials have expansion coefficients like this, some larger than others. Steel is .00065. The change in length of the forty-foot wall with a 30°F change is (.00034 x 40' x 30°F) / 100°F = .0041 feet or approximately one-sixteenth of an inch. Somewhere in the length of the wall, you would expect a small one-sixteenth of an inch crack or lots of hairline cracks that add up to one-sixteenth of an inch you can't see. Now it's winter, 10°F, when summer was 100°F—a ninety-degree change, so a three-sixteenths of an inch crack or lots of small cracks would be expected. Where would you expect the cracks to occur in the wall? If you have a perfect wall and all joints in the mortar are the same, then as the wall gets bigger, you would expect to see it halfway in the middle of the wall. However, if you're pulling on something, where does it break—the weakest link or the skinniest part? So if you have a four-foot window in the wall and remove the masonry where the window is, instead of being ten feet tall, the wall is effectively six feet tall with some masonry over the top of the window and some masonry under the window. You have a ten-foot section changing to a much smaller section. You would expect to see the cracks somewhere around the window. Some cracks in masonry are expected, and this does not mean the wall is structurally unsound. This type of temperature crack gets wider when it's hot and closes up when it's cold. Most people never see them anyway because there are usually a lot of small cracks instead of one big crack. If the crack gets bigger and bigger, then there's something wrong with the wall like it's moving or settling. Anyway, masonry walls always need a foundation to support them. The taller the wall, the bigger the foundation.

Okay, you have a foundation for this brick wall and you start laying it up. How high do you lay it up before you start attaching it to the framing, and how often do you attach it to the framing? Most building codes will tell you to use something like one tie fastener to the framing for every 2.7 square feet of wall. Personally, I like ties on every wall stud spaced sixteen inches on center vertically. Think of how high you could stack bricks up without them falling over. Of course, the thicker the wall, the higher you could stack them, and laying them in mortar helps considerably, but only after the mortar sets. Most brick veneers are one wythe thick or nominally four inches. That being the case, most masonry walls are laid up in around four-foot lifts, the mortar sets overnight and the ties connect the wall to the framing, and then you can lay up more. If the distance from the foundation to the wood framing is too high, the brick wall will need piers to reinforce it or be two or more wythes thick depending on the height. Most codes recommend load-bearing masonry walls to have an unsupported height-to-thickness ratio of 12:1. That means four inches thick can be forty-eight inches tall before it's tied to something, or one foot thick can be twelve feet tall. That's just about what you would find if you stacked them up until they fell over.

Brick or masonry walls are virtually maintenance free if installed properly. That's why they're one of the best exterior finishes and most common throughout the world. Keep in mind that brick walls are not waterproof. Small amounts of water will penetrate them, and the wall design needs to allow for the water to get out. There is usually an air space of at least one inch between the back of the brick and the structural sheeting on the house. This keeps the water from reaching the house, and it runs down the back of the brick to the lower course where there should be flashing and weep holes to force the water back to the exterior. Flashing and weep holes should also be over windows and doors where it's possible for rain to hit the brick wall. All good masons know about this and how to install quality brickwork. Brickwork also offers the opportunity to be creative in the exterior walls with arches and reveals and setbacks in the face of the brick.

Cement stucco finishes offer a lot of the same benefits as masonry and have been used for almost as long. Stucco is typically between one and two inches of thick cement and can be applied over masonry or wood framing. It can be applied directly to the masonry, and it needs a metal lath attached to the plywood if it's used on wood framing. The exterior appearance looks the same. Stucco also needs joints for movement, and the locations of these joints affect the appearance. The locations of the joints should be known before the stucco is applied. Stucco also needs the same type of flashing and weep holes as brick. Stucco requires the use of skilled craftsmen to install it; your regular old sheetrock finisher can't do it. You will find very old stucco houses with tile roofs throughout the world, and these houses require little maintenance on the exterior, which is probably why they last so long and are so popular.

Everyone probably knows something about wood siding on a house. You just fasten the exterior wood to the structural framing. The types of wood for the exterior finish vary with different places. Some of the most common are cedar, fir, pine, redwood, cypress, and the list goes on. There are basically two ways to install wood siding; the boards are vertical or horizontal. I prefer vertical with a board and batten type finish. Some people like it horizontal with a shiplap type finish. Some people like it diagonally. Good carpenters know how to install wood siding on a house. I recommend using wood boards as long as possible to minimize the joints in the wood. Especially if the boards are vertical, try to use one board from eave to first-floor line. The exterior surface texture of the boards can be smooth or rough-cut; it depends on what you like. The wood should be attached to the house with hot-dipped galvanized or stainless steel screws or ring shank nails. If you do not use these types of fasteners, the nail will rust and a rust streak will appear on the wood surface over time. Wood exterior finishes have been used since man has been able to cut trees. Wood will not last as long as masonry, but with proper maintenance, it will last several lifetimes.

I think a combination of the above materials offers the best exterior finish. I prefer wood or stucco above the eave lines in gable spaces. You don't have to cut each brick at the roof slope intersection, and it's easier to build. This is especially important if the brick cannot start at the ground and continue up to the eave. Sometimes contractors bolt a steel angle to the wood framing and set brick on this; that's not good practice unless the steel is strong enough by itself to carry the masonry.

Vinyl and aluminum sidings are seen more and more. These sidings are installed in a way similar to wood, except the attachments are a type of clip. These clips do not offer the same strength as nails or screws; however, they provide enough strength to hold the siding to the framing. These types of siding do offer a longer lasting finish than wood. You do not have to paint or stain it as often as wood. Some offer a lifetime warranty on the finish. There's something about the flimsiness of the material that worries me though. It's not the material I want as a security barrier. This issue can be eliminated by using a strong plywood backing behind the siding or the original wood siding.

The various other materials used for exterior finishes, such as metal, are rare, but I have seen it. Copper adds some nice touches if used appropriately. However, to me, metal siding looks like a barn. Fabric siding looks like a tent and offers the same lack of security. Certain rooms like sunrooms or partially enclosed rooms lend themselves to fabric, and believe it or not, fabric is becoming more and more acceptable as a roofing and siding material. This is not for me. Give me masonry or wood.

One thing that has always amused me is the idea that brick siding houses don't burn like other siding houses—it's better in fires and you get a better fire rating for insurance purposes. It's true that brick does not burn in a normal house fire. However, all things burn or melt if the fire is hot enough; think of lava. It takes sheetrock awhile before it will burn, and it's used as a fireproofing material. What difference does it make if the wood framing burned and left the brick wall still standing? That's not the problem anyway; when the wood burns enough, it pulls the brick over. If the house burned enough so that only the brick was remaining, it would be a total loss anyway. If your house is going to catch on fire from the outside, it would be better if the exterior is a noncombustible material like brick. Most houses catch on fire from the inside and usually around the kitchen. It could be something about grease being combustible when it gets hot. By the way, if the pan of grease catches on fire, don't try to pick it up and throw it outdoors. Most likely, it will spill on your hand, the scars will scare small children, and you'll have to learn to become ambidextrous for a while. Just put a lid on the pan or use a fire extinguisher or stop the fire some way without setting yourself on fire. Heck, stack bricks on top of the pan.

There is a new fad going around that I don't understand. The experts recommend that the house be wrapped with a waterproof membrane before attaching the siding. Think plastic. For centuries, houses have been built without this membrane. I do not see any need for this wrap. First, you have to nail the plastic to the house with enough nails to keep it in place until the siding is attached. This usually involves many nails that punch many, many holes in the material. Then the siding attachment puts more holes through the wrap. So you have a hole every sixteen inches both horizontal and vertical. How can that be waterproof? They say it also keeps the wind from entering the air-conditioned interior of the house. I say, if the wind can get through the exterior finish, then the plywood sheeting, then the insulation, then the sheetrock or interior finish, the wrap with the holes is not going to stop it. If you feel like you need a waterproofing layer behind the masonry, use a paint-on type (with no holes) applied to the plywood sheeting. I recommend a layer of felt paper between layers of wood. This prevents squeaking as much as anything when the wood moves against each other. That's why they use a felt layer between hardwood floors and the subfloor. Anyway, if you want to, or the code officials say you have to, then go to the expense of wrapping your house in plastic.

When you're planning your house, be sure that you see some drawings that show the exterior elevations of your house on all sides. You can play with these drawings to see the different looks of the various sidings or combinations of each. With today's computer-aided drafting, it's easy to change the drawings from brick to wood and so on. Spend some time on the exterior elevations until you settle on the way you like it.

Chapter 8
Stairs, Ramps, and Elevators

Helical wood stairs

If you have a two-story house or more, and I don't recommend a house more than one story, you will need stairs or ramps and/or elevators. I would say that at least one half of all houses have a second story. It makes good sense when you think about the same roof and foundation for two floors.

It makes no sense if you can't walk up them and need an elevator to get to your bedroom. I guess, the older people get, the less they like stairs; I know I have grown not to like them.

Stairs

Stairs can be a grand feature in a house with great architectural impact. They can be strictly practical like spiral stairs or ladder stairs. Most of the time, they are functional with some architectural detail, such as fancy spindles and curved handrails attached to them. Whatever type of stairs you need, they should be comfortable to climb. I know if your son is going to put his brother in a box and slide him down the stairs, you need them to be steep. The steeper they are, the harder they are to climb, but the faster your son's brother slides down them.

Although stairs have been around forever, recently the building codes have seen fit to dictate how the stairs will be built in your house. The codes will also dictate to some degree how the handrail will be and the spindles if you use them. So let's get the code requirements out of the way. Most codes require a stair to be three feet wide and have a slope so that two risers and one tread added together must be between twenty-four and twenty-six inches. The risers cannot exceed a certain height, usually seven inches. All the risers must be the same height on any one stair from floor to floor. The spindles must be close enough together so that a four-inch diameter ball cannot fit through them. The risers are the vertical part of the stair, and most are between six and eight inches. The treads are the horizontal part of the stair and are usually around eleven inches wide; codes require they have to be eleven inches in most cases. Therefore 7 + 7 + 11 = 25 inches and the code is happy.

You have to have at least one handrail if the stairs are over thirty inches high. The height of the handrail is given by the code for the stair and the stair landings and is usually thirty-six inches high. The pickets are to be four inches apart so when your infant child is playing on the stairs, he or she will not be able to stick his or her head through the pickets and get hurt. Be sure to check the local code for your area.

Personally, I like stairs to be as comfortable as practical. That is, the lower the riser, the better. Two four-inch risers would dictate a tread of between sixteen and eighteen inches. You could take nice little steps and experience the climb. If you have a long way to go up, your stairs would be very long and not too practical in the interior of a house; they may be okay in your yard or if you're only climbing twelve feet. The area the stairs take up in the house is figured as follows. Let the floor-to-floor height in your house be ten feet. Ten feet is 120 inches, and eighteen risers 6.67 inches tall is 120 inches. Each riser would be about 6 11/16 inches, and they have to be the same height. There is always one less tread than there is riser, so there will be seventeen treads, and let's say they are eleven inches wide. The length of the stairs will be 17 x 11 = 187 inches or fifteen feet seven inches. Your stairwell is three feet by fifteen feet seven inches for a 6.67/11 stair. If you use 4/16 stairs, the stairwell would be three feet by thirty-eight feet eight inches. If you used ten-inch risers (10/11), the stairwell would be three feet by five feet six inches. If you have ever been to Thomas Jefferson's Monticello, the stairs in his house are approximately eight-inch risers and nine-inch treads. He wrote that he did not want to use up space in the stairwell, so he made his stairs steep. The caretakers of Monticello will not let you use the stairs. They say they're too steep and people will hurt themselves. Most people use a stair that is 7/11 inside the house and less than that in their yards and porches.

Pull down, sliding stairs, or hidden stairs are usually used to access the attic space in most houses. Some houses just have an access hole in the ceiling, and you need a ladder to get into the attic. If your attic is framed correctly, there should be storage space or space for the mechanical systems in your house. You will need to get into the attic occasionally. Unless you have direct access into the attic from a floor or permanent steps, the pull-down stairs is the way to go. Locate these out of sight in a closet or hall if possible. There are different types available; there are commercial and residential types, and there are narrow and wide ones. I recommend a wide, commercial, heavy-duty type. It makes it easy when you have to get into the attic and carry things in or out.

Ramps

Ramps are becoming more and more common, especially with the ADA (Americans with Disabilities Act) requirements that are now law. It basically states that there can be no barrier that would prevent a disabled person from using a public building the same way a person that is not disabled uses the building. This act is bleeding over into the private residential housing section.

Ramps help to change elevations when walking or rolling, and the law says they have to be on a 1/10 slope maximum. That is one foot vertical for every ten feet horizontal. If you have to go up ten feet, you would need a minimum of a hundred feet of distance. Also, every thirty feet, the ramp has to have a flat area big enough for a wheelchair to rotate, so they take up a lot of room. If you have a person in a wheelchair, I would not build a two-story house for that person.

Elevators

Elevators are the way to go if you have to change floors. There was a time when elevators were cost prohibitive for residential construction. But, over time and with the help of modern machines, elevators, while still pricey, are showing up more and more in houses. You will always need a stairway in case of fires and things like that, but modern elevators are just cool, especially a fast one in a house.

There are basically two types of elevators, hydraulic and friction. Hydraulic types are like the machines that lift a car up in a garage. They have a cylinder that fills with hydraulic fluid and moves the cab up and down. They require a space to store the fluid and pumps, and they require a hole in the bottom center of the elevator shaft for the cylinder ram to be placed. Because of the length of the rams in the cylinders, hydraulic elevators are rarely over four stories. These types of elevators are the slowest kind because it takes time for the oil to be pumped into and out of the cylinders.

Friction elevators are run by cable, pulleys, and winches. The cable is wrapped around the winches, and the winches are raised and lowered by an electric motor. I think they get their name from the friction between the cable and winch. These elevators usually require a penthouse at the top of the shaft where the motors and winches are usually located. That's probably why they are seldom used in houses. These elevators are extremely fast, if you want them to be, exceeding 350 feet per minute. It takes a couple of floors for an elevator to reach that speed, so residential elevators will not be as fast as building elevators.

If you are going to have an elevator, it should hold at least two people at a time and be as quiet and as fast as possible. It should have a phone in it, so if it breaks, you can call for help. For residential, a high-quality hydraulic should do the job, but there are new electric ones hitting the market, so check them out and always have the manufacturer of the elevator install them.

One other thing about elevators is the shaft. The shaft should be soundproof and fireproof. On two walls of the shaft, the guide rails for the cab will be attached, usually at the floor elevations. The elevator shaft has strict dimensional tolerances that must be kept in order for the cab to slide properly on the rails. The openings for the cab can be in the other two walls. Having openings on both of the other walls substantially raises the price of the elevator. Some people like to enter the elevator on one wall and exit from the opposite wall, or sometimes access restraints require you to open on both walls. At the bottom of the shaft is the elevator pit. This pit is usually a minimum of eight inches deep and can be as much as four feet deep and should have a drain in the bottom in case water or fluids get into the shaft.

So if you are going to have two or more floors in your house and there are going to be old people or people who can't climb stairs, an elevator is the only way to go. If you are a blind person in a wheelchair, and you build a two-story house, be sure the cab will allow the wheelchair to rotate 360 degrees and that the buttons you press have brail numbers.

Exterior concrete stairs

Chapter 9

Exterior Trim Work

Exterior trim work can get fancy.

The exterior finishes and trim work are usually associated with the cornice at the eave line and the woodwork around the windows and doors. This topic also includes the ceilings in the porches, woodwork around decks, and everything decorative on the outside of your house. As you can imagine, this decoration can be as plain or as fancy and complex as your taste will allow.

Unless all of these decorations are made of concrete or stone, such as on the Biltmore house in Asheville, North Carolina, they will have to be maintained and painted. With this in mind, I like my exterior finishes simple and plain and easily maintained. I have seen some houses that remind me of a gingerbread house with all the stuff they hang on the exterior. It all depends on what you like. Keep in mind that on the exterior of the house, insects and the like really enjoy the complex finish work. Anything that creates nooks and crannies will be filled up with all kinds of living nuisances, from spiders to bees to bats and whatever is indigenous to the area your house is in. All of these lovelies will build their houses or nests or webs directly attached to yours. So if you like piano-key corner molding, use it inside of your house and not under the overhang at your eave. Trust me, unless you live in the desert, all of those piano keys will fill up with some type of bug that will discolor the paint or eat the wood and just love the nifty little house you made for him. He probably will even think his piano key is the right note.

Exterior trim is necessary on most houses, so a little planning here can go a long way in keeping you happy with your masterpiece. For example, if you have an exterior ceiling over a porch or deck, the ceiling is most likely going to be made of some type of wood, such as plywood. Rather than starting on one side and nailing up the four-by-eight panels in a row until you get to the other side, you should plan the ceiling layout with the lights and ceiling fans and trim and the location of the joints in the plywood and the like. Once the ceiling is thought out and the lights and things are symmetrical, you could even make a statement with the ceiling by painting some mosaic on the ceiling or doing some neat wood layout with board and bead lumber. A ceiling that is not thought out and planned looks unbalanced and odd. Plan the layout of the ceiling so it is in sync with the house.

Exterior ceilings need to be thought out also.

Using shutters as an exterior trim has always bothered me, unless they're real and actually work and need to be there to protect the windows during a storm or for security. To me, nailing fake shutters on the side of a house to pretend they're real makes no sense. However, I'm the first to admit that I do not know "pretty"; so if you like these types of shutters, go for it. Another thing that bugs me is fake windows in the roof area that give the impression that there's a room behind the window. I call these types of windows doghouses. They usually just stick out from the plane of the roof and are just big enough for one small window. There will usually be a pair of these or more. They don't do anything except eventually leak. I guess they're pretty to some people.

Exterior trim, such as handrails and posts on decks and porches, is an opportunity to show the true quality of the construction of the house and to truly make the house inviting and warm. A nice, strong, sturdy handrail will imply the same about the house—especially if the handrail is well constructed with concealed nails or screws and is sanded or routed smooth at the edges. There's nothing worse than a handrail that's so wobbly that you know you'll fall through if you lean on it, especially if it's on the second floor. One of those grand, old, strong type rails with the fancy pickets and elaborate corner trim around the posts is a comforting thing. With the right furniture and wind chimes, it can even be soothing, especially while sipping Kool-Aid and watching the kids play with the spiders who have built their web between the posts on the porch.

Anyway, the exterior trim on a house is a necessary thing and should be thought out. This type of thought can convert a regular front door into a grand entrance or a deck into a work of art. Use the best type of exterior wood because it is on the outside of your house and exposed. There are more and more composite type materials for use on the exterior of a house. The ones I have seen are much denser than wood and do not float. This material tends to be much more expensive than wood but the manufacturers claim that it lasts longer and does not decay or get eaten by termites. It hasn't been around long enough to really know for sure. Interior trim wood like white pine does not last very long on the exterior of the house unless it is well maintained. The exterior trim should be attached better because it goes through a much tougher service life, such as hot and cold, the weather, and kids hitting the house with a baseball. Lumberyards, especially those that specialize in windows and doors, have a wide variety of exterior trim. The good ones even carry it in treated wood. Check out all the different types of moldings and pick out what you like. Keep in mind, most people are going to see only the decks and doors on the outside of your house, while on the inside, they will usually see everything. Therefore, money spent on fancy interior trim work makes more sense than money spent on exterior trim that is seldom seen. But it's your money, so do it your way.

Chapter 10

Plumbing, Fixtures, and Hardware

In plumbing, I am including sewage, potable water, gas, and all other types of piping. This could also include oxygen or other gasses or liquids. I know that most houses do not have those types of things, but they are available if you need them.

The plumber is one of the most important people you will have working on your house. The foundations, framing, and plumbing are very difficult to change. Correcting anything that goes wrong is expensive and unpleasant. Think of sewer gasses. Get to know your plumber and accommodate all of his reasonable requests if possible. Sooner or later, you will need to work on a water heater, and it's best to have the pipes accessible so you will not have to tear out walls to get to them. If you let the plumber have some input into these items when they're installed, it usually makes it easier to fix if they break.

I know you do not want to hear about things that break or leak. If your plumber tells you he does not have leaks, he's probably not doing any work. Leaks are inherent in plumbing; you just fix them if they occur. The plumbing lines are always pressure tested prior to getting them approved. Any leaks that happen during the test are fixed. When the plumbing is finished on your house, there should be no leaks that are known. Over time, things wear out, break, dry out, or work themselves loose, or they could have been defective. There will need to be some adjustments on any plumbing system. These things usually happen during the warranty period for the work. That's why it's important to use a reputable plumber who won't be gone next week.

Sewage

Sewage is the waste that you flush down the drains and toilets in your house. All of these sewer pipes converge to one location and tie into the sewer main that takes the sewer to your own septic tank system or to a public utility. Most plumbers' work stops five feet from the exterior of the house. That is to say, they will cap off their pipes after they have installed them out five feet from the house. At that point, the site utilities take over and run the sewer to the sewer tap or septic tank and the other pipes to their taps. Sometimes if the distance is not too long, the plumber will run the lines to the taps. Usually there are water, sewer, and gas taps, and each of these taps is an extra fee from the permitting authorities along with the permit for the house. Sometimes these fees can get very expensive, especially if the local utilities are trying to control the growth of houses in a certain area.

Sewage pipes are normally schedule 40 PVC pipe or other types of plastic material. Sometimes sewer pipes are run in cast iron. This type of pipe is much quieter than plastic; therefore it is used for vertical stacks of pipe to minimize the sound of the sewage falling in the pipe. If you insulate the PVC, you can accomplish the same thing. Either way, if you can eliminate the sounds of the sewer pipes, it is best to do so. The size of the pipes depends on how many fixtures they are draining. The more toilets, tubs, washing machines, and sinks, the larger the size of the pipes. The length and slope of the pipes also contribute to the size of the pipes. A normal three-bedroom, three-bathroom house usually will have a four-inch diameter sewer line leaving the house.

Sewage, like water, runs downhill. Therefore most sewage systems use gravity to move the sewage through the pipes. When gravity is used, the slope of the pipes becomes critical. You may think the more slope on the pipes the faster the sewage flows and leaves your house, so that's good. However, you do not want the pipes to have so much slope that the liquid runs off and leaves the solids. The solids have to be suspended in the liquid to flow. Also, waste lines have to have air to work properly. Turn a two liter coke bottle upside down, and it will drain very slowly as it tries to gulp air to relieve the backpressure from the atmosphere. If you punch a hole in the bottom of the bottle and then turn it upside down, it flows right out.

The same principle applies to sewage lines. The pipes penetrating the roofline in your house are usually vent pipes that tie into the sewer lines. You should have a vent on the upstream side of every fixture that drains into the sewer. Usually, in the attic, these vent lines are combined into one or more before they penetrate the roof to minimize the number of holes in the roof. All sewage pipes must have clean-out fittings. The plumbing codes require them at certain locations. I think you should have more than the code requires. They are inexpensive, and if you need them, they save a lot of work unstopping drains. Most drains are stopped up by hair build-up over time, although other things can stop them very quickly.

All waste lines have a P-trap that holds water to prevent the sewer gases from going through the pipes and into your house. The water in the P-traps stops the gas. The P-traps need to have water run through them often enough that the water in the trap does not evaporate and the trap becomes empty. If you have a toilet or sink that you will seldom use, you will need to flush it or run water in it every so often to keep the P-trap full. You will be able to smell when the P-trap is empty. The vent pipes will help with most of the smell but not all of it. Empty P-traps are not the plumber's fault, and neither are defective interior parts of exotic water faucets. Sometimes you just have to change out the faucet or the interior parts. Do not get me wrong, most master plumbers' work is leak free and you never see the plumber for twenty years. Then again, his neighbor's son might have needed a summer job, and he let him install your European gold-plated faucet art with all the attachments, and now it has that slow drip leak that drives you nuts. The plumber will probably tell you that you should have bought American. Tell him you know that, but to please just fix it.

If your house cannot use a gravity flow sewage and you need to have a pumping system, be sure it's designed by a professional engineer who's experienced with these types of systems. If you need one of these systems, your house is probably lower than the surrounding terrain. You are in a hole. The way this system works is the sewage in your house will gravity flow to the lowest point in the system. That point should be outside of your house with some type of holding tank in place. In the holding tank there will be float switches that will turn on when the sewage gets to a predefined level. The switch will turn on a pump that will pump the sewage uphill to a point of another pump station or to an elevation where gravity flow can take over. There should be a backup float switch and alarms so that if the system ever broke, you would know it. These systems usually have emergency generators in case the electric power goes out. If you can avoid it, you do not want one of these pump systems. However, pumping stations are used in most public sewer utilities to get the sewer over hills or if the lines are too long and flat.

Water

The water pipes in your house are usually PVC too, although they can be copper or steel. If you do not have your own well, then you will be buying your water from the local water utility. This utility will install a water meter, usually at the edge of your property where the water mains run. The plumber or site utilities contractor will run a water line to your house. If the pressure is too great from the water utility main line, you will need a pressure-reducing valve to lower the pressure in the pipes in your house. If you do need a pressure-reducing valve, I recommend that you install an outside faucet above the pressure-reducing valve in order to have a water line with full pressure. The pressure in your house is usually around 60 PSI. Sometimes in your main lines, especially if you are at the end of the street, the pressure can be double that to 100 PSI or more. Having one line with that much pressure can be fun when you're squirting the kids or a dog or cleaning the driveway.

There should be a main cutoff valve at the area where the water lines enter your house. This valve should turn off all the water in your house. You should know where it is and be able to get to it easily. Once the water enters your house, the line will split up and go to the fixtures and appliances that use water. At every fixture or appliance, there is a cutoff for that item. One split will go to the water heaters that you have. The cold water will go to the water heater and then hot water to where it needs to be. Some people have more than one water heater, and some people have instant hot heaters that do not store hot water but heat it through a manifold as you need it. Those instant hot heaters are expensive (several thousand dollars). I have never used one in my houses, but I understand that they work well and you never run out of hot water. There are new types of plumbing systems that work so that you have a main control box located in your house, and a line runs from this box to each appliance or fixture. This is supposed to allow you to have equal water pressure to all the different places at the same time. I have never used one, but I hear they work too. Water pressure and volume of water at each fixture are dependent on how much the pressure is as it enters the house. The size, length, bends, elbows, and the quality of the plumber's work also determine the water pressure and volume at each fixture.

The water lines in your house should be thought out prior to the plumber starting the hole boring process. The plumber and the carpenter framer should get together and be sure that there is adequate access in the walls and floors for the plumbing lines, and that there are not any conflicts with framing members and fixtures and appliances. Having a floor joist directly under the outlet for the tub or toilet does not work, and this can easily be avoided with a little planning. Also, the plumber should be able to run his lines as straight as possible. Every bend or elbow in a water line decreases the pressure at the end. The width of the wall needs to be larger than the plumbing lines that will be inside of them. A normal two-by-four wall is three and a half inches wide. A three-inch pipe will not fit inside of it. Usually, pipe is measured by the inside diameter for pipe sizes up to twelve inches. So a three-inch pipe will be three inches, plus the wall thickness of the pipe, plus the fittings that connect the pipe together. Walls with plumbing lines should be at least two-by-six or more. After the walls are up is not the time to find out the plumbing will not fit in them. One other thing, a two-by-four wall that has water lines will have holes bored in it to allow the water lines to be installed. If you use two-by-four walls and drill a one-and a-half-inch hole in it, you do not have a two-by-four anymore; you have a two-by-two.

To simplify the plumbing in your house, think of this. You will need water coming to your house under enough pressure to work your appliances and fixtures. There needs to be a valve to turn all the water off going into your house. There needs to be a valve to turn the water off at each appliance or fixture. These valves are usually in the sink cabinets or behind the toilet, etc. All of the appliances and fixtures will have exposed faucets that you turn on as you need water. The homeowner usually picks them out, and they range from inexpensive to ridiculous. Once you use some water, it will have to be drained out through the sewer pipes, and those are the ones with the vents and P-traps. The sewer pipes are not under pressure, and the wastewater flows through them by gravity. One thing that should never happen is connecting water pipes to drain pipes. Condensate lines or any lines associated with the potable water that drains into the sewer should have an air gap or check valve to prevent the sewer from stopping up and back flowing into the water line. An air gap is simply a gap between the end of one pipe and the start of another. When you fill a bucket up with a hose, the air gap is the distance from the end of the hose to the water. If the hose is under the water, you have no air gap.

I have been mentioning appliances and fixtures that need water and waste. To give you an idea of what I'm talking about, the following are some examples. The water heater needs a water supply and a drain line for the overflow and blow-off valves. Some refrigerators need water for ice and drinking, and some need a drain line. Heating and air conditioners need drains for the condensation and drain pans. Of course, sinks, tubs, showers, toilets, and dishwashers need water and drain lines. Some cook tops, ovens, and heating systems need gas lines. Floor drains in laundry rooms or shower rooms need drain lines. All of the appliances and fixtures, along with the hardware that goes with each, have to be picked out by the owner, and this information needs to be given to the plumber. Or, you can let the builder pick it out and hope you like it. I am sure that most of the women reading this understand the importance of the kitchen appliances and bathroom fixtures. With regard to women, these two rooms tend to make or break a house. That being said, I recommend that you start looking at these appliances and fixtures and the hardware associated with each as soon as you start the house-building process. There is a lot to decide on, including self-closing toilet seats.

While you're picking out the fixtures, hardware, and stuff, keep in mind that the cost associated with plumbing at today's prices is in the range of $400 per fixture. This price includes the material and labor for the pipes and fittings used to get to each fixture location. The material would be CPVC lines, and if you desire copper, the price would be higher. Fixtures with just water and no sewer lines, such as exterior regular hose bibs, a refrigerator with just an icemaker, a garbage disposal or dishwasher, are usually counted as half of a fixture. Whirlpool tubs or showers with fancy, multiple water jets are counted as two fixtures. Main sewer and water lines that run to your house are in the range of ten dollars a foot for sewer and four dollars a foot for water. The fixture cost, along with the hardware that goes with it, is not included in this $400 per fixture. Fancy toilets, tubs, sinks, and faucets get very expensive. At the local home supply store, you can compare these prices to regular fixtures and hardware, and at the specialty plumbing fixture shop, you can see the prices of unusual toilets, exotic sinks, and solid brass hardware.

Of course, the plumbing will have to meet all the code requirements that have to do with plumbing and water. The local plumber should know all of these. However, the government keeps getting more and more involved with your house to the extent that you now have to use "water saver, 1.6 gallons per flush" toilets. The old toilets used around three gallons per flush. I guess somebody in the past figured out the right amount of water you need not only to flush the toilet but to run down the lines right. I don't know what happened, but the law now says that you can only have toilets that use one and a half gallons of water per flush. The government probably gave somebody a grant to study this, and they came up with the idea that one and a half gallons will work. I guess it all depends on certain amounts of certain things, and most people tell me they just flush the toilet twice. I also heard of a friend of my cousin's brother-in-law who put in the code-required toilets, and after he got all his occupancy certificates, he bought some old toilets and replaced the new ones with them. I don't care much for the new toilets either, and I can think of better things the government could do than mess around in people's toilets. I mean, why should anyone care how much water you need to flush? There are not many things worse than a toilet that's not flushed properly, except maybe a government bureaucrat who thinks he needs to stick his nose in it. Anyway, the local plumber should know such matters.

Chapter 11

Electrical and Lighting

To keep up with the times, I should call this chapter Proof that Atlantis Existed or something clever like that. It seems the electronic world changes almost daily. Just when I was getting used to the radio and big plastic records, little plastic records and 8-track tapes came out. Then cassette tapes, then CDs, DVDs, Blue Ray, and thank goodness my hearing is wearing out and is not so delicate that I need the latest high-fidelity systems to be happy. Not that it makes any difference, because we are back to radio from a satellite. You can call up any song any time you want on the Internet, and the headphones are so gross you can bust a move with them. Wireless and tiny is the big thing now. I remember when the battery for a cell phone was as big as a 12-volt car battery and it had its own case. You hardly ever heard of someone losing his phone back then. Now the phones and batteries are so small, it amazes me how they can last much longer and work better than those heavy 12-volt jobs. And to put it mildly, my kids do everything on their BlackBerry, and we no longer even have a home phone. Before we got rid of the home phone—and by the way, we had to have call forwarding, backwards, sideways, answering, messages, mailboxes, enjoy the music while your party is located, and then you hear rap crap from hell before they tell you your party cannot be located so leave a message after pushing 1, or push 2 and leave a call-back number, or push 3 to page this person, or just wait on the beep to speak, and after you speak, push 2 to hang up or just hang up, all for only $1,150 per year, the warranty service and actual phone are extra—I watched as the conventional code of social behavior while using the phone changed over the years.

The first phones were party lines where you had to be careful of what you said because someone could be listening. For some reason, you always waited for the phone to ring a few times; I guess so people would not think you were just sitting by the phone waiting for it to ring. You only had one phone, and even if you were walking by it right when it rang, you would wait a couple of rings and then answer politely. Since you only had one phone, you only had one wire to that phone. Back then, the phone company would install that one wire and give you a phone and come to your house and fix it if it broke. Then came private lines and multiple phones and multiple wires to every room in the house, even in the bathroom. Somewhere along the line, answering the phone became more important than life itself. At one time, it was dangerous to be between the phone and my daughter when it rang.

In the old days, when the phone rang, it was "I wonder who it is" while you waited for the proper number of rings, which evolved to a death cry of "I'll get it," followed by a mad dash to the phone. Then came remote-control phones. These are phones that do not have a wire between the part you hold and the part that you put the part you hold in when you're not holding it. Then, you could have the phone with you constantly when in your house, and not lose a second between when it rang and when you answered it. Not only that but you could get beeped and talk to two or more people at once, which brings me back to phone etiquette. It seemed that every time someone told me to "hold on" because they "got a beep," my phone would somehow cut off. So I decided that I do not need to talk to people who put me on hold and that these people were usually the ones who talked on the phone very loud, very often, and anywhere they had service. Now we have phones so complex that we do not call them phones any more. These things are so small and powerful that you have an entire typewriter keyboard and TV picture screen within an area the size of a credit card. You can record volumes of pictures, music, numbers, names, games, and access the Internet for your e-mail or make just a simple phone call if your fingers are not too big to mash the keys. All of this with no wires anywhere except for the battery recharger to an electrical outlet when you need it. There is one thing to keep in mind. It seems we are back to where we started with the etiquette and politeness when using the phone. I think, because people are texting more and because you never know who is listening again or looking at your e-mail, you better be good for goodness sake.

So how many wires do you need for the phone system in your house? Do you still want or need a hard wire phone in every room? I do not think we will ever do away with the cell phones we have now; therefore, you do not have to wire for phones in every room. If you feel better running a phone wire to every room, then do it. Phone wires and phone jacks are not that expensive, and you do not have to have a phone at the end of every phone wire. I do recommend running a computer wire to every room in the house, and more than one in some rooms.

I used to know the names for the types of wires, but they changed so fast I just say the "computer wire" and that's the wire for the computer. The electrician can tell you what the correct technical name would be, such as Cat5. The phone wire is for the phone, the TV wire is the cable, the speaker wires are for the speakers, the video wires are for the video cameras, the wires for the exterior flood lights are for the exterior floodlights. Things that still need wires need the right ones, and your electrician should be able to tell you the right size and name for the various wires you will need in your house.

Keep in mind wireless does not end with just the phones. The music system has wireless speakers. The security system has wireless contacts that they say are better than the ones with wire because you do not have wires you can short circuit. There are wireless doorbells. Your computer systems are now wireless, including the keyboard, mouse, monitor, printer, and just about everything. I guess eventually all you'll need in a modern house are electrical wall outlets and lights with the wall switches. Even the switches can be clap-on and clap-off deals. So we are down to lights and power. That does not seem like too much to deal with. It also makes you wonder—in ancient times, did they evolve into an entirely wireless society? Think about this.

The ancient people evolved to a completely high-tech, micro, wireless state and recycled everything and such. That's why we don't find things like phones and TVs in archeological digs. The great libraries were reduced to tiny, removable hard drives that you plug into your completely biodegradable phone. If our history goes back to Noah and the great flood, then we have arrived at where we are in 5,000 years. Think about mankind before the flood, from Adam and Eve until the flood or about 5,000 years. Why would they not be more advanced than we are today, say like the mythical Atlantis?

Electricity

Let's start with the electrical power in your house. I think you could say it's right up there with water as far as importance in the house. Everywhere you need water and in places you do not, you need electricity. I think everyone over six years old knows that electricity and water do not mix. In fact, I do not think electricity mixes with anything, and I certainly do not recommend trying to mix it with something you might spill on you. I will be the first to admit I do not know that much about electricity, and I am afraid of it. I know some electricians who joke about it and work on the outlets while the wires are hot. Some electricians will even touch two hot wires to show you it doesn't hurt. These guys go in the same category as the people who insisted Wonder Dog could not be a real cop when you were a kid. Don't hire these guys to wire your house.

Electricity will be one of the first things you will need to start building your house. It will be supplied either through the use of temporary power brought to your site by the electric company or by portable electric generators. It is much better to get the temporary power brought to your site as quickly as possible and preferably before the construction starts. Usually the electrician will install a post with an electric meter on it and a breaker box with some outlets to plug power tools and lights into. Once the temporary post and meter is set, the power company will bring power to the meter. The power will be in the form of wires either overhead on poles or underground. Overhead is free, and underground costs extra in most areas. Some neighborhoods already have the power underground, and the cost for this in the cost of the lot. The power company electricians are the only ones who get to access the electric meters.

Once the house is completed, the power company will install a meter on the exterior of the house. The location of this permanent meter should be worked out with the electric company and you and the builder. It should be where the power company can read it easily, and in a place that's not an eyesore for the house, but it should not be too far away from the main circuit box in your house. After the house has been approved by the building official, signifying that it's ready for the permanent power to be turned on, the power company will come and switch the power from the temporary meter to the permanent meter.

The cost of the electricity you use to build your house will usually show up in the general conditions line item of the detailed cost estimate for your house. (More on detailed cost estimates later.) Some of those electricians who were concerned about kids' knowledge of the police force will say you can straight wire the temporary electric meter straight to the house to test the house and bypass the permanent meter. This is when you find out why there's a main circuit breaker and more importantly the color of electricity. First you hear this loud boom and a big fireball comes out of your house right before everyone who is working there comes running out threatening to murder the moron. Although most of the fireballs I have seen have been blue, I have been told that they can be any color. I think electricity is blue, but I don't think it really matters. The good electricians will usually tell everyone that the main power is going to be turned on at a certain time and date. I like to think that this evolved from there being a spirit of professional courtesy among the craftsmen, but it's probably to avoid payback. I would not be honest if I did not say it's extremely funny when this happens, especially if someone jumps out of a second-story window, but only if no one got hurt and it was truly an accident.

Once you have determined where the power meter will be on the exterior of your house, the location and size of the main breaker box will be next. The largest and most expensive wire in your house usually is the one running from the electric meter to the main breaker box in your house. That is why you try to put the meter and main box close together. I highly recommend this wire be copper (some people use aluminum). The main breaker box is just that. How big your house is and how much electricity you need now and in the future will determine the size of the main breaker box. There are many sizes, but small houses usually start at a hundred amps and go up from there to 200 amps then 400 amps and on up. If your house requires more than 400 amps, you should have an electrical engineer assist you in the electrical plans for your house. If your house has 400 amps or more, you probably will have more than one main breaker box.

In each main breaker box will be the main breaker, which is usually the largest in the box and at the top or bottom of the box. Smaller breakers feed off of the main breaker and are in the body of the box. From the main breaker box, the wires will spread out all over your house to everywhere you have electricity. The more electricity a certain appliance requires, the larger the wire will be. Having the main breaker box close to the electric dryer, stove, hot water heater, or furnace will save on the cost of the wires. Just like with the HVAC systems, the main breaker box needs easy access and some room around it to work on when or if you need it. Appliances that require a lot of electricity, such as the dryer, stove, hot water heater, and furnace, will have one wire running from the main breaker box to that individual appliance. That wire will have its own breaker in the main breaker box.

There can be several wall outlets and lights on one breaker. These are usually grouped by the rooms the breaker serves. The doors of the main breaker box usually have a list of the breakers by number and a description of what the breaker supplies. For example: Breaker 1—Master Bedroom Lights and Outlets; Breaker 2—Hot Water Heater; Breaker 3—Oven in Kitchen. The list of the breakers should be written legibly and explicitly regarding what each breaker is connected to. I call the breaker and what it is hooked to with the wire a circuit. Everything that uses electricity will require a certain amount of amps. The breakers are rated by the amount of amps it takes to trip them. For example, if the toaster needs ten amps and the hairdryer needs fifteen amps and they are both hooked to the same circuit with a twenty-amp breaker, then the toaster and the hair dryer are running at the same time the breaker trips. That probably would be in the morning while you're cooking breakfast while getting ready for work on that special day when they evaluate your performance for the big promotion. This is a simplified scenario of what circuits and breakers are and how things are wired.

The building codes require certain circuits be certain ways. Certified master electricians know how many amps are needed for each circuit and all the code requirements. One thing a certified master electrician cannot predict is how many Christmas lights you plan to plug into one outlet. I think that's determined by whether or not Lowes had that sale running when you finally broke down and went Christmas tree shopping or how serious you are about the neighborhood prize for best house or front door.

Okay, we know we have a good electrician and all the code requirements are met. We know that one end of the circuit wire is going to be where the main breaker box is located, but what about the other end of the wire? That's where you will need the juice (wall outlet) or where you will turn the juice on (wall switch). The codes have a minimum number of required wall outlets and lights, but that minimum number is hardly ever enough for the discerning housewife. The only way to be sure you have it right is to take a set of the house plans and lay out the furniture and everything that will need electricity. Then make sure there is a wall outlet within three feet of the appliance. I never could understand why they always put wall outlets low down on the wall. The last time I remodeled, I put the wall outlets at three feet above the floor. The electrician did not have to bend over to put them in, and I do not have to bend over to plug into them. We both liked it better.

Now that the wall outlets are located, we need to locate the lights and the light switches. Again, take a set of the plans and draw where you want the actual light bulbs to be. Don't forget outdoor lights, under-counter lights, attic lights, nightlights, indirect lights, fish tank lights, and lamps. The switch for each light now must be located. I like pull chain switches for attic lights; most people want wall switches. If you have a light and you want to turn it on or off from two different places, it is a two-way switch. It takes twice as much wire as a one-way switch. The same thing goes for a three-way switch and up. You can have several lights hooked to the same switch, such as several can lights in a row. Some people like to be able to turn all the exterior lights on from one place in the house. Some people like to turn them on from several places, and that would make them two- or three-way switches. Only you can decide what type of switch you want for each light, appliance, and ceiling fan.

Most switch and light locations are simple. A closet light goes in the center of the closet, and the switch is by the door. Most closets have a single door and only need one switch and one light. Most bedrooms are just a large closet with the light switch by the door and the light in the center of the ceiling. If you have a ceiling fan with the light, you will have a duplex switch at the door, one for the light and one for the fan. If you have more than one door for the bedroom, you will need two-way duplex switches at each door; then you can turn the light and fan on or off from either door. Some people like dimmer switches on all the lights. Dimmer switches allow you to adjust the brightness of the light from all to nothing. If you use dimmers, be sure to get high-quality ones, because they tend to break more often than regular switches.

Additionally, the color of the wall plates for the switches and outlets needs to be picked out. They come in all colors, shapes, textures, and material. I suggest the standard ivory or beige. You can always change out the switch or outlet cover plates for an individual room later. Each light fixture must be selected as well. Even can lights have a wide variety of exterior lenses to choose from. The selection of light fixtures seems to be limitless. Because of this, most builders set aside an allowance of so much money for all the lights and fans. If you go over the allowance, you owe them more; if you do not spend all the allowance, you owe them more. It's funny how that works. Just kidding. However, the allowances usually are not enough to cover all the lights you want. So have the builder shed some light on the allowances during the light of day.

Chapter 12
Heating, Ventilation, and Air Conditioning

Heating is to Minnesota as air conditioning is to Florida, very important. I have found that where people were born and reared has a lot to do with the amount of cold or heat they find comfortable. I grew up in Loris, in northeast South Carolina, seven miles from the North Carolina line and fifteen miles from the Atlantic Ocean. I saw enough snow to speak of only once in my childhood, and it lasted a day. I remember because the schools shut down, and we had a holiday. It was manna from heaven.

In 1979, I spent the winter in Cohassat, Minnesota, erecting steel on a coal-fired power plant owned by Minnesota Power and Light Company. Just for your information, the Mississippi River begins in Cohassat, and you can walk across it there. If I never see snow again, it will be too soon for me. I flew into Duluth, Minnesota, in early January, dressed in my winter clothes. Due to the amount of snow on the ground, the plane could not pull up to the concourse, so we walked through a four feet wide, hundred-yard long path cut through the snow to the building. The snow was over my head, and when I got to the building, I knew my windbreaker would not pass as a winter jacket.

The company I was working for, Kline Iron and Steel, had rented a car for me. I think it is now standard for car rental places to ask if you have ever driven in snow before they let you have one of their cars. When I put the first car I was given in reverse and went back a few feet, a big blue fireball came out from under the hood. That and the loud bang scared the remaining heat out of me. The rental agent asked me if I unplugged it. I asked if it was an electric car. In case you didn't know, up north they have plug-in electric heaters to keep the oil and fluids from freezing. Makes sense now. After I unplugged the second car, I got in and put it in reverse, and then I could not make it stop until it hit the car on the other side of the parking lot. There is something about brakes and ice that doesn't mix and takes getting used to. I ran into the exit gate that has the arm that raises up to let you out of the parking lot while trying to drive the third and last car the rental company could see fit to rent me that day. I did not argue with them too much. I called the job, and they sent a driver out to get me and gave me a company truck to drive to work the next day.

I got up bright and early the next day in order to be the first at work. I was driving along a two-lane highway that had been snowplowed and everything was going well until I came to a wreck in the road. Cars were backed up about ten long on each side of the road. Just off either side of the road, the snow looked like a smooth, white blanket laid out on the ground for as far as you could see. It looked like a nice, flat, white asphalt parking lot—or at worst, I thought, a cotton field with maybe a few rows to deal with. I couldn't understand why the cars didn't just go around the wreck on the side of the road. Not wanting to be late for work, I pulled the truck onto the shoulder so I could go around. Then, before I could say it, and I almost did it, I had gone down an embankment and the truck was submerged in fluff snow. I crawled out of the driver's side window, climbed onto the roof, and stuck my head and shoulders above the level of the white death. All the people and the highway patrolman were running toward me. The trooper yelled at me, "Didn't you see the poles?"

I was thinking telephone poles, and there weren't any, so I said, "What poles?" I think the trooper saw the grits running out of my mouth and realized I was freezing to death in my winter clothes. He politely pointed out to me that the sticks on the side of the road have numbers on them that tell you how deep the snow is—just in case some idiot doesn't know it snows more than an inch in Minnesota. During my whole time in Minnesota, I could not stay outside for more than two hours at a time. My body would freeze from the inside out. I met some of the hardest working people in my life there. They could work from sunup to sundown in the snow, and it didn't bother them. The foreman of one crew told me about his summer vacation to Myrtle Beach, South Carolina, in August of one year. He said he couldn't stay outside in the heat and humidity for more than two hours, and he was sunburned the whole time. Some like it hot, and some like it cold. So depending on the location of your house, you will need some heat, some cooling, or some of both to keep yourself comfortable.

There are many ways to heat and cool your house: solar, thermal, gas, electricity, water, and all kinds of heat exchangers. These systems take the heat out of the air in the summer and add heat to the air in the winter. All of the various systems have their own unique requirements, such as exhaust chimneys, condensate pans, air intakes, condensers, fans, filters, and so on. The local HVAC man can fill you in as to what normally works best in the area you are building in.

The most common is a unit centrally located in the house that has ducts that supply heated or cooled air to each room and a central return duct to recycle the air back to the unit. This is known as central air conditioning. Big houses are split into zones, and each zone in the house will have its own unit. You will need to tell your HVAC man how you like your house to be. Some people like instant heat or cooling. Some people do not like to hear any sound from the systems and want a constant temperature everywhere. The HVAC man can size your system up or down according to your likes. Personally, I like to feel the hot or cold air blowing out of the vents with minimal sound.

The size of the air handling system (fan) and ducts will determine how fast air moves out of the ducts. The size of the heating or cooling unit (furnace) will determine how hot or cold the air is. For some reason, HVAC people use the word ton to measure how much air conditioning you need; the more tons, the bigger the system. There is the old rule of thumb for determining the size to use. For a normal average house, they say you need one ton per 400 to 600 square feet of heated space. For 2,000 square feet, you could figure a four-ton unit. The airflow in this system should move at around six miles per hour (500 feet per minute). This would be like a slight breeze that would make leaves rustle. If you held a dollar bill up to the vent, you should see it move with the breeze. All houses are different, and depending on how well it's insulated, the number of windows and doors, the ceiling height, and other considerations, the sizing of the HVAC system needs to be designed accordingly. What I have just said is a very simplified approach. The actual design of a proper system requires calculations by an experienced HVAC person. If the system is very complex, a professional mechanical engineer would be needed to determine the right amount of tons and the size of the ductwork.

One thing to keep in mind about whatever system you use in your house is that sooner or later you will need to maintain the system, even if it's just to change the filters. I highly recommend that while you're designing the house you include the HVAC people in the process. Ductwork requires chases that sometimes cannot be hidden in the walls. Sometimes the walls need to be wider than the normal stud size to accommodate ducts and piping. The location of the unit should be in a place where a person can access all sides of the unit. Eventually, a time will arise when the unit needs working on or replacing. If you cannot get to the unit, it becomes very difficult to work on. I have seen units put in the crawl space under a house, where you had to crawl on your belly to change the filters. I have seen them in the attic with houses with low slope roofs so that a normal size man could not fit around it. It's best to design the house with the unit location in mind so that an area is set aside for the system and the duct runs are preplanned. Allow at least three feet around the unit. Also, be sure the area around the unit is floored and the access to the unit is floored. It helps to have a light with a plug-in outlet over the unit too.

If you preplan for the system and accommodate the HVAC peoples' desires, the cost should be less. If the HVAC people have to squeeze a unit in somewhere and the duct runs are going in all directions and around your elbow to get to the room, it will be reflected in the price of the system. At today's prices, a normal, typical system for a normal, typical, average house runs around $3,000 per ton for new work. This price includes the material and labor to install the system. It does not include the running of the electrical wires to the system or hooking up the system to the wires. That's usually in the electrician's price.

I have greatly simplified the HVAC systems and everything associated with it. There are many things that need to be discussed and planned, such as humidity control, condensation, thermostat controls for the system to turn them on and off, and the list goes on. There are certain things that are safety issues that should never be allowed to happen; for example, dryer vents should never run uphill, and gas exhaust vents should never run downhill.

The HVAC people can fill you in. The days of turning on the attic fan and opening the windows, or building a fire in the fireplace, have gone the way of the dinosaurs. Although I do like a good attic fan with the cool breezes or a nice warm fire, I'm glad there are no tyrannosaurus rexes running around. So tell your air condition man how hot or cold you like your house before the system is installed. Install it where he recommends and allow enough area around the unit to maintain it properly.

Chapter 13

Insulation

Thermal Insulation

Insulation is one of those things that I'm not sure how it works. It doesn't let the hot or cold or sound transfer through the wall, ceiling, or floor. Take a thermos jug, for example; I understand that the good ones have a vacuum between two layers of walls, and the hot or cold cannot transfer through the vacuum. Insulated windowpanes have a vacuum between the layers of glass. So why do we stuff the voids in the floors, walls, and ceilings with various types of insulating material? Most likely because we can't create a vacuum economically in these voids. Nevertheless, even the best thermos jugs do not last much longer than a day. The ambient temperature always wins in the end. However, it is a proven fact that houses with insulation require less energy to heat and cool. The more insulation, the less energy needed. Since insulation is relatively inexpensive and is a onetime cost—compared to electricity and gas, which are never-ending costs—it's one of the best values in your house.

Even the best insulation will not be effective unless the house is being framed so that the wind can't find cracks and loose joints to sneak through. A house that is framed right will not let wind find a way into the interior, particularly at the eaves of the house.

There are code requirements and recommendations for the amount of insulation required in the floors, walls, and ceilings. They have assigned a thing called an "R" value for the amount of insulation you need or are required to have. Some people use a "U" value, which is the inverse of the

R value. Anyway, the higher the R value is, the better the insulation. The R value goes up with the thickness of the insulating material. It's sort of like if you're sleeping and you get cold, you put a blanket on. If you're still cold, you put another one on, and so on. The question is, how much should you use? The answer is, as much as you can get in the space available. For floors, the most you can get is the depth of the floor joist. The same is true for the walls. For the ceiling, you can pile it on until it touches the roof rafters, if you like.

Depending on the part of the country you live in, the local builders usually know the required R values for that area and normally insulate at least to those R values. There are different types of insulation. There is Styrofoam, high-density Styrofoam, fiberglass, cellulose fiber, cork, shredded paper, cardboard, wood, and the list grows each year. Each material has its own claim for how well it insulates.

All insulation except for the Styrofoam tends to consolidate over time and lose some of its R value. Most attics use a spray-in type of insulation that I personally do not like, but they say it's the best because it covers everything and goes everywhere—even where you don't want it to. Spray-in insulation is the same material as blanket insulation except it's in a loose form like fluffy cotton. If you use the spray type in the attic and the attic is also used for storage, the insulation dust tends to get on everything in the attic. That's why I don't like it. I like the fiberglass paperback type that lies in between the ceiling joist. You can roll out several layers in the attic if you like. The pink panther will like you, too.

Insulation works if it is installed properly. Most insulation comes in sixteen- or twenty-four-inch wide rolls or pieces. This is because most framing is sixteen or twenty-four inches on center. All of the voids must be filled completely. This will require handwork between all the studs, joists, doors, and windows that the voids are too narrow for a standard piece of insulation to be installed in. The insulation must be attached to the framing, usually with staples, so that it does not move or slide down due to gravity. If your house is framed properly, there will be no airflow through the floors, walls, or ceilings. The insulation stops whatever airflow the framing did not. Some builders install Styrofoam four-by-eight sheets on the exterior of the house. I prefer for the house to be sheeted with plywood and for the insulation to go between the studs. If you use two-by-six studs on the exterior, you would get five and a half inches of insulation. Just be sure that the craftsmen who are installing things in the wall do not pull the insulation out while they're installing pipes or wires. The insulation should be installed after all the other trades are finished with the walls, ceilings, and floors. Pulling the insulation out usually does not happen except for when something is changed after the insulation is installed. Insulation is very itchy. Most people don't like to get it on themselves, which is why it's usually the last thing done before the sheetrock.

Sound Insulation

Sound insulation is different from thermal insulation. It's more dense. Most builders use thermal insulation for sound insulation and it works, but not as well as the dense sound type. The plumbing waste pipes should be sound insulated, especially the vertical ones. Some people like certain rooms soundproofed for obvious reasons. Nobody over 18 wants to hear rap music when you're trying to listen to Jimmy Hendrix.

Water pipes and HVAC ductwork should be insulated if they're outside of the conditioned house envelope. In other words, if the water pipes are under the house and you live in an area where it gets cold, these pipes will freeze. If the water pipes have to be installed like that (that's very bad construction), they must be properly insulated with pipe insulation or they'll burst and flood you. Hot water pipes can be insulated to keep the water in the pipes hot, but usually they're not in residential construction. I do not recommend insulating hot water pipes unless they can freeze. HVAC ductwork should be insulated not only for heat loss but also for condensation. This type of insulation is usually covered by the plumbing and HVAC contractors.

Insulation is usually installed by the square foot and the thickness or R value. Typical values for fiberglass batts for floors and walls are R = 13, and for ceilings R = 30. The installed cost for insulation ranges from fifty cents per square foot and up. Half of that cost is for the material, and half is for the labor.

Once again, insulation installed properly works. Use as much as you can and at least the minimum R thickness for whatever type you decide. Inspect the insulation just before the sheetrock is installed to be sure there are no cavities anywhere, especially around doors and windows. This brings me to one last word on heat loss. Most of it occurs through the doors and windows. So the more doors and windows you have, the less insulated walls you have and the higher the energy bills. Floor-to-ceiling glass walls make no sense to me because you don't look out of the bottom or top three feet of the glass unless you're lying on the floor or standing on a ladder.

Chapter 14

Sheetrock and Interior Walls

By far, most residential interior walls are covered with some type of Sheetrock. Sheetrock has many names depending on what part of the country you're in and to whom you're talking. I suppose the technically correct name would be gypsum wallboard. As this name implies, Sheetrock (that sounds stronger than gypsum wallboard) is made of gypsum and paper or cardboard. Gypsum is a combination of various ingredients but mostly of sulphate of lime with water for crystallization. Pure gypsum is known as alabaster.

Gypsum is hard and relatively lightweight. It's fire resistant and is used for fire proofing in some applications and assemblies. Sheetrock should not be used where it could be exposed to weather or moisture. They make a type of Sheetrock some people call green board that has water resistance properties. Technically it's called a type X core gypsum wallboard. Most builders use this green board in bathrooms and around sinks and areas where water could get on the walls. They paint right on the green board, but over time, with moisture around, the paint flakes off. When you go to the painter and tell him the paint is peeling, he'll tell you that you have a moisture problem and it isn't the paint's fault. That is true. Although using green board in these conditions is done quite commonly because it's cheaper, there are better products to use in these areas than gypsum, such as cement board, lath and plaster, or ceramic tile. Sheetrock, if installed and finished properly, is great for most of the other walls and ceilings in the house.

Sheetrock is manufactured by pressing gypsum and other ingredients between two layers of paper to form a smooth, flat sheet. Sheetrock comes in sheets of various thickness, widths, and lengths. Depending on the ingredients and physical properties, Sheetrock can be made to carry structural type loads. Sheetrock can be used to brace the wall framing it is attached to and provide diaphragm type action; however, most engineers and builders conservatively neglect this bracing attribute. At one time, gypsum boards were made thick enough to be used for roof sheeting, but the problem gypsum has with water ended this practice.

Today, most Sheetrock used in residential work is one-half or five-eighths inches thick. It's attached to the wood framing with screws, nails, or sometimes glue (rarely). Glue is most often used to attach Sheetrock to other walls, such as brick or block or other layers of Sheetrock. The framing is usually spaced sixteen to twenty-four inches on center. One-half-inch thick Sheetrock is used for sixteen-inch spacing and five-eighths-inch thick for twenty-four-inch spacing. The Sheetrock is usually attached to both sides of the framing except in areas like attics where only one side is needed. Multiple layers of Sheetrock are used on a stud wall if sound or fire ratings are needed. The sheets of Sheetrock are usually four feet wide, although, I am told, you can special order custom widths if you're willing to pay the extra cost. I do not recommend special ordering Sheetrock. The length of the sheets runs from eight feet to sixteen feet in even feet. Most Sheetrock for residential work is going to be one half inch thick by four feet wide by eight or twelve feet long.

The installation of the Sheetrock involves several steps to arrive at an acceptable finished wall or ceiling. To begin with, the framing that the Sheetrock is attached to has to be strong enough to carry the weight of the Sheetrock and the live loads that would make the framing move. This is especially true for ceiling framing that also acts as floor joists for the second floor. One of the properties of Sheetrock is that it does not stretch, and that's not good. In engineering terms, it should not be put into tension. When Sheetrock is used as a ceiling under a second floor, the weight of the people and furniture on that second floor might cause the floor joist to deflect or sag and thus crack or open up the joints in the Sheetrock. We know that if this sag does not exceed the length of the floor joist divided by 360 (360 has no units), the Sheetrock should not crack or open up. You have to be careful with this empirical formula, because as the length of the floor joist gets longer, the sag gets too much. Usually in residential construction, the lengths of the floor joists do not exceed sixteen feet. If they do exceed sixteen feet, I recommend changing the 360 to 600, and you will get a much stiffer floor.

Example: sixteen feet equals 192 inches; 192 inches divided by 360 equals approximately one half inch. If the floor joists are designed so that they won't sag more than one half inch with the weight of the people and furniture on them, the ceiling should not crack. Accordingly, twenty-four feet divided by 360 equals approximately one inch, and twenty-four feet divided by 600 equals approximately one half inch. It's difficult for people to see a half-inch sag, but most people can see a one-inch sag. It's good practice to design the floor so that it doesn't sag more than half an inch or the length divided by 360, whichever is less, under the full live load. This is good not only for the Sheetrock but for appearances also. Most codes only require the length divided by 360 for floor live load deflections. As stated above, this may be too much under certain conditions. Remember, codes are minimum requirements and not necessarily the best guideline in some areas, such as floors.

Other requirements for the framing besides strength (don't forget, as Hardy Cross said, "strength is essential but otherwise unimportant") are square, plumb, level, and straight. When the Sheetrock is installed to the framing, any imperfections in the framing will show up in the Sheetrock. If the wall is bowed, the Sheetrock will be bowed; if the wall is leaning out of plumb, the Sheetrock will be out of plumb; if the corners are not square, the Sheetrock will not be square. Usually if the Sheetrock installers see that the framing has some inconsistencies, they'll fix the bad places by shimming out the areas with dead wood or try to fix the areas with the finish process. Most qualified framers know about the necessity of square, plumb, level, and straight, and this usually is not a problem.

While we are on the topic of framing, it is not the framers fault if the Sheetrock is placed in the house all in one spot and the framing is racked out of square, plumb, level, and straight by the gross weight of the Sheetrock. Gypsum Sheetrock weighs four pounds per square foot for every inch of thickness. If the Sheetrock is stacked twelve inches thick, the floor would be loaded to forty-eight pounds per square foot. Most codes require live load, floor rating for residential construction to be forty pounds per square foot. The Sheetrock should be loaded into the house so that the required number of sheets for each room is placed in that room and no more, unless the Sheetrock weight is checked out against the framing. This is true not only for Sheetrock but for other building materials as well, especially roof shingles.

The Sheetrock is attached to the framing with screws or nails. When using either one, you do not want the screw or nail head to rip through the paper cover on the Sheetrock. You want a slight depression around the head so the head will be covered up in the finishing process. The spacing of the fasteners varies according to whom you talk with. I recommend not exceeding twelve inches on center for walls and eight inches on center for ceilings. Although this is not a requirement, it's good practice for the sheets to be installed perpendicular to the framing. The ceilings should be installed first in a room and the walls second. To minimize the joints, and thus the finishing of the Sheetrock, the longest sheets possible should be used. For walls longer than four feet, the sheets should be installed horizontally across the wall framing.

The joints at the Sheetrock edges should be as tight and close together as possible. The sheets should be staggered so the joints are not continuous. Needless to say, but anyway, everything that goes in the wall must be in place prior to installing the Sheetrock. This includes all electrical, mechanical, plumbing, insulation, blocking for cabinets, trim, and everything that gets concealed in the walls. Getting concealed in the wall can become a problem. All the things that protrude through the Sheetrock, such as light switches or wall outlets and HVAC vents, have to be cut out of the Sheetrock. Good contractors mark on the floor where the locations of these things are so that after the Sheetrock is installed they can make sure that none of these things remain concealed. If you do not have some way to locate these things, they are extremely hard to find after the Sheetrock is up. The cutout around the items is important also. If the hole is too big, then it's patched during the finishing process and it's difficult to make it look pretty. It is surprising to watch experienced Sheetrock hangers mark and cut out the holes and see how accurate they can be.

The exterior windows and exterior doors should be installed prior to hanging the Sheetrock. The house should have at least temporary lights and some type of heating or cooling as required. Sheetrock installed in the wrong environment tends to mold very quickly. It's important to control the environment of the Sheetrock during installation with fans or heaters as required. Using the permanent HVAC units to do this is normal, but be sure to use heavy-duty filters with these units to keep the Sheetrock mud dust from getting into these units. Under certain conditions, it's okay to install Sheetrock if the exterior windows and door are not installed. However, this is risky due to rain, and it's very difficult to control the environment. The potential for mold increases, or the mud might not dry quickly enough and can even freeze. I highly recommend the exterior door and windows be installed prior to the work involved with the Sheetrock. The Sheetrock is the beginning of the finish stages of the house construction, and in order to protect the finishes, the house should be locked after construction hours anyway.

The finishing of the hung Sheetrock involves several steps. The material used is joint tape and joint compound or mud. The first step is sometimes called the bed joint step. This is where all the fasteners and large open joints are filled in with the mud. The next step is called taping and is where the joints are covered over with a paper tape and more mud. The edges of the Sheetrock are slightly depressed to allow for the fasteners and finish material to make a smooth surface over the joints. Sometimes the paper tape is replaced with a fiberglass mesh or other material, if the joint requires more than the normal paper. If the Sheetrock has been hung properly, these first two steps are combined into one step called bedding and taping. This is usually what happens. After step one is allowed to dry, it is smoothed off by sanding with sandpaper or wiping with a moist sponge. Then another layer of mud. Then drying. Then smoothing off. Then another layer of mud and so on until the Sheetrock is finished. People ask me how many layers of mud are required. The answer is until the wall looks pretty, pretty, pretty.

True professional Sheetrock finishers require fewer layers and less mud and less sanding or smoothing, resulting in less of a mess to clean up. Rookie finishers are a complete disaster. The mud is all over the floor and tracked everywhere from their lack of tool control. The dust from the sanding, because of their use of too much mud, is on everything and will saturate the air for months, clogging up the air filters in the HVAC units. One way to tell the difference between a pro and a rookie is by age, and another is to look at the hand tools of the people. If the tools look used from wear and tear, but are still clean of the mud buildup, the person is a pro. If the tools are caked with mud, beware and get ready for the mess.

You should not be able to detect the joints or fasteners in properly hung and finished Sheetrock. Let me qualify that by saying that when you inspect Sheetrock, it should be with lights that are similar to the lights that will be in the room when the construction is complete. Also, you should stand three to five feet from the wall when you inspect it. I have seen people place a flood light directly against the wall, shining up the wall with their face a nose length away. I also know a guy who claims to have a four-foot diameter magnifying glass that he uses for inspections. Needless to say, these people are cursed with this need to find imperfections, and they are doomed to a life of disappointments brought on by their unrealistic approach to residential construction. Houses are not built in heaven, and they are not perfect, but you still should not be able to see the joints or fasteners in a properly finished wall.

There are three areas of cost in Sheetrock. There is the material cost, which includes the material, delivery fees, the Sheetrock itself, all the fasteners and metal trim and edge moldings, along with the mud and tape and sandpaper, etc. There is the cost to hang the Sheetrock and the cost to finish the hung Sheetrock. Material costs vary, but one half inch of Sheetrock with the mud and fixings costs around thirty-five cents per square foot delivered. If your house is at some isolated location or not on paved roads, you can expect the Sheetrock delivery cost to be a separate item; and depending on the location, it can become expensive. A truck full of Sheetrock is going to be one of the largest trucks to bring material to your house. It is usually a specialty type of truck with a unique crane attached to facilitate the stocking of the Sheetrock in the house. The use of this crane saves a lot of time and labor, and if the sheets of Sheetrock have to be hand carried into the house, the price of delivery goes up. Also, because the truck is so large, it requires a solid, firm road to run on. I would not try to bring a fully loaded Sheetrock truck down a steep, wet, dirt driveway unless you know a good wrecker service. Labor cost to hang the Sheetrock for normal houses is around thirty cents per square foot. Labor costs to finish the Sheetrock is around forty-five cents per square foot for normal houses. Things that would not qualify as normal are curved walls or ceilings and tall walls or high vaulted ceiling that would require scaffolding to get to the work. Some Sheetrock subcontractors like to price the job by the sheet. For every sheet they hang and finish, they get a certain price. I do not recommend doing this. A lot of the sheets tend to get cut up and never hung. These sheets wind up in the dumpster, and you wonder why the estimate for the number of sheets needed was so way off, especially when you have to go buy a dozen more sheets and hand carry them into the house.

One last thing about Sheetrock is that the buckets that the mud comes in are very handy. There are usually several of these buckets at the end of the job, and you may want to keep some of them.

The remaining walls and ceilings in the house are going to be made of various other materials. Second to Sheetrock would be wood. The wood can be in the way of paneling or single boards. This wood paneling can be as lush or plain as you like. Think of walnut paneling in the study or office. Wood walls and ceilings require a skilled finish carpenter to install the wood without butchering it. This is extremely important if the wood is going to be stained or clear varnished. If the wood is going to be painted, then the use of wood putty and caulking can forgive a lot of bad cuts. If the wood is not painted, then the joints have to be tight or it will look ugly. One other thing about wood is that it shrinks. Although the joints are tight at the end of the installation, they will open up over time. How much the joints open up is totally dependent on the moisture content of the wood when it's installed and the moisture content or humidity of the house over a few years. The lower the moisture content and the higher the heat is in the house will cause the wood to shrink more. Wood is much more expensive in both labor and material cost than Sheetrock, and that's why it's not used as much as Sheetrock. To me, wood looks better than Sheetrock, but there is much to be said for a smooth Sheetrock wall with wood molding and trim.

Other types of wall finish are stone, hard tile, marble, ceramic tile, and more. These are covered in the following chapter on ceramic tile and stone.

Chapter 15
Ceramic Tile and Stone

Bathroom with ceramic tile

When you need a demanding, impervious, and easily cleaned lining on ceilings, walls, and floors, tile and stone are about your only option. Tile is manufactured all over the world from various ingredients, including mixtures of clays, shale, feldspar, and flint. It is standardized in some countries with regard to finishes and sizes, but tile comes in all shapes, sizes, patterns, and colors. Ceramic glazed tile is used most often in residential bathrooms, kitchens, laundry rooms, and rooms where water and cleaning are needed for the walls, ceiling, and floors. Tile has been used for ornamental purposes dating back to the Egyptians and perfected by the Greeks and Romans. Ceramic mosaic tiles are readily available in almost unlimited patterns from most tile suppliers. Then there are the custom one-of-a-kind mosaics of them. Because tile is unique to each manufacturer, it is best to consult the manufacturer's literature for available sizes, shapes, thickness, trim pieces, accessories, and colors.

Nowadays, tile is installed pretty much the same way everywhere. It is bonded to cement board that is attached to the framing by screws or nails. This board is made of a type of concrete with synthetic additives and fibers to allow the concrete to be pressed into sheets. This board has good natural resistance to water damage. Most contractors use sheets that are at least half an inch thick and thicker. This cement board has almost taken the place of the old way of installing tile. The old way is with lath and grout beds. The results of both ways are to provide a strong, smooth, water-resistant surface to bond the tiles to. There are pluses and minuses to both the old and new way of building this surface. The only difference is that with the use of premade sheets, the walls have to be straight. The sheets do not bend. If you have curved walls and ceilings, you have to use the lath and grout. Also, tile accessories that are inserted into the walls, such as soap dishes, toothbrush holders, toilet paper holders, etc., are easier to insert in lath and grout bases. For the cement board, you should build a wood backing for the cement board to attach to around these accessories. Whatever the base is for the tile, the supporting structure must be stiff enough that it does not move enough to crack the tile. Tile is not very forgiving when it comes to movement. A minimum sag or deflection of the span divided by 600 is required. Even stiffer is better and recommended.

When it comes to tile cracking, it will. It's just a matter of time. It simply cannot stretch or flex. Usually the tile will crack in the joints, most likely at the corners, and the cracks are so small you cannot see them—although sometimes, a crack will go through the face of a tile. The size of the tile helps in minimizing the cracks. Bathroom shower floors usually have small tiles; the smaller, the better. Wall and ceiling tiles are usually larger. The larger the tiles, the more likely you are to see a crack, especially on tiles that are more than twelve inches wide. When floor tiles are installed over a concrete slab on grade, usually any crack that develops in the concrete will telegraph through to the floor tile. It is best to let the concrete cure for at least thirty days or longer before installing a tile finish. If the concrete has cracked, you must use a thin, latex-type bonding compound on top of the concrete to minimize the possibility of the crack developing in the same place in the tile.

If there are any intentionally made joints in the concrete, such as expansion or control joints, there must be a joint in the same location in the tile. If the concrete floor moves, the tiles are going to move and will usually crack. That goes to say, with any floor under the tile, if the floor moves, the tile cracks. Be very careful when using a wood floor under tile. As we know, wood, by its nature, has to move. Be sure the wood framing is over designed and extra strong under a tile floor, especially one that has large, open spaces. In a small powder room, it is usually not a problem unless you have used those expensive, special-order mosaic big floor tiles that take six months to get. Then you probably will get a crack in the worst possible place if you built it on wood. All you can do is say the wood grunted and found its final resting place, chip out the cracked tile, put another in, and hope it doesn't grunt again. If wood or concrete floors are built properly, it usually takes several years (if ever) for a crack to show up in the tile. Also, just because a crack shows up does not mean the construction is faulty. If a crack shows up and continues to grow, that's another story. I recommend using the cement board on the walls and ceiling, and for the floor, use the grout bead, especially in the shower floor. If the cement board is used over wood for the floor, be sure the wood is over designed and as stiff as you can make it. Do not allow any bounce or movement in tile floors.

Tiles are attached or set to the sub base (the cement board or grout bed) with cement grout or synthetic mastic, or a combination of both. This mastic must be firm enough and sticky enough to hold the tiles in place, especially if the tiles are set in the walls or ceiling. One way to determine if the mastic is mixed right is to take some on a trowel and turn the trowel sideways vertical, and if the mastic sticks to it without sliding off, it is mixed properly.

Prior to attaching the tiles to the sub base, the layout or position of the tiles on the floor, walls, and ceiling should be established and agreed upon. This is especially important if mosaics are used or special trim pieces. Special trim pieces are considerably more expensive than regular flat tiles and are usually used as accent jewels in the walls. These jewels need to be thought out prior to setting the wall. If you have a good set of plans, the designer will have already done this layout. Without plans, someone has to decide how the joints and trim will look on the floor, walls, and ceilings. If you use different size tiles on the floor than the walls or ceiling, this needs coordination to line up the joints. Also, the joints need to be as symmetrical as possible so that you do not have a wide tile on one side of the room and a narrow, skinny piece on the other side of the room. Most good tile setters will snap a few control lines on the sub base so that the tile will look right when he's finished and to minimize cuts around protrusions through the tile work, such as faucets, shower heads, and toilets.

The size of the spacing of the tile, or the joints in the tile, needs to be established. Where there's a lot of water, such as a shower, the joints should be as close together as possible. In other locations without a lot of water, the joints can be as wide as you like them. Some people like wide joints with the joint grout a special color. You just have to work out what size joints and what color joint grout with the tile setter. I do not recommend the joints to be wider than three-eighths of an inch. I personally prefer as small as possible joints. The tile setter will use plastic spacers at the corners of the tile to space them uniformly when he's setting the tile on the sub base.

The tile is set on the sub base by first applying a layer of mastic with a toothed, flat trial and then mashing the tile into the mastic. This requires skill and experience by the tile setter to be sure the tile surfaces are set in a smooth plane. If a tile is mashed lower than the adjacent one, then the surface becomes uneven. Some unevenness is to be expected, but it should not be noticeable. When the tile is set and mashed into the mastic, it should have a full bed of mastic under the tile. If there are cavities under the tile, it is more likely to crack and will make a hollow sound when tapped on. Once the tiles are laid, they are allowed to set for at least twenty-four hours.

After the tiles have set, the grout is squeezed into the joints with a rubber edged float or sponge. It's important to make sure that the grout has completely filled all the joints and cavities in the tiles. The excess grout is wiped off the surface of the tiles, leaving the joints filled to the surface of the tile. The grout is allowed to set usually for twenty-four hours, and then it's cleaned with a mild solution of muriatic acid or white vinegar. It's very important to clean the tiles with something that will not discolor the grout or tiles. The tile setter should always try out a small area with the cleaning fluid to be sure the fluid does not affect the tile. Usually the tile setter knows what's best for the grout he's using. If the tile setter is good, there will not be much grout for him to clean off anyway.

Stonework and tile are the same when it comes to setting them, so everything above applies to stone and tile. Stonework is usually seen on floors. It can be used on walls and ceilings, but there's not as many ornamental pieces in stonework as in tile work. They say that stonework discolors more easily than tile, especially if harsh chemicals are used to clean them. I have not cleaned enough to know for sure, but it makes sense, because tile has a hard baked-on surface and stone does not. I can see where a stone like polished marble could change color more easily than tile.

I recommend tile or stone for all bathroom floors, laundry room floors, and the walls in the bath areas around the showers and tubs. Some people like tile floors everywhere, which is fine with me too. Tile makes a fine floor. It's just a little cool to the touch sometimes, and it's not very forgiving if you drop glass items on it. In certain parts of the world, it's the only flooring considered. With the exception of the bedrooms (where carpet is king), you see tile and stone floors more and more in all the rooms in the modern house.

Chapter 16

Floors

I don't recommend dirt floors for houses. I do recommend dirt floors for caves, barns, foundries, potato mounds, and some latrines.

As most people progressed from dirt floors in their dwellings, I believe the next logical step would have been different types of brick and raw stone. Next would have been cut stone and concrete. Once mankind started building off the ground, wood came into play.

For today's floors, you have concrete slabs on grade, or concrete slab on grade with brick, tile, stone, wood, carpet, or any type of finish, even, I guess for some places in California, dirt. Think about it; California may like a sod house with dirt floors. I hear they don't burn, and if they slide down a hill, you can just pile them back up into your house. Or, you can have wood floors built a minimum of twenty-four inches off the ground that support wood subfloors and wood finish floors. Or you can have wood framing that supports any type of finish, the same with steel. Linoleum-type floor coverings provide the same type of water protection as tile and stone and are used in the same places. They offer a wide variety of colors and patterns and have been used successfully for many years. They do not have the durability of tile or stone and show wear, especially in areas where you stand in the same place a lot, such as in front of the washing machine or sinks. They are more economical than tile or stone, and they can be replaced with tile or stone when they wear out if the framing is strong and stiff enough for the extra weight of the tile or stone.

The floors in a typical house match the type of framing of the house and the climate of the area. Basement and cellar floors are concrete with or without a finish. In the South, houses with a concrete slab on grade with various types of finishes are popular. Houses with crawl spaces usually have wood framing with wood, carpet, or tile finish floors.

Whatever type of floors you use in your house, when you walk on them you want them to be level and not bounce, especially if they are slab on grade.

Slab on grade floors, if built properly, seldom have problems. To build a proper slab on grade, be sure the slab elevation is at least twelve inches higher than the surrounding grade. Also be sure that the surrounding grade drains water freely and quickly away from the house and does not pond up around the perimeter of the house or try to flow into the house. The subsoil under the concrete slab on grade should be granular (sand or crushed stone) so that any moisture in the soil has a natural barrier to allow the moisture to move sideways and not up to the slab on grade. The subsoil must be compacted to a compaction density that will prevent settlements or consolidation of the soil. We could talk about soil compaction for a long time, but if you say you want all the soil—both virgin and fill material—to be compacted to 98 percent Standard Proctor, you'll be fine. What this means is that you want the soil to be compacted the best it can be, until it almost can't be compacted any more. Standard Proctor is a type of test that is used to test the compaction of the soil. If you are of the Clemson persuasion, you would say, "Compact the hell out of it."

If the water table is close to the ground surface, concrete slab on grade floors are not recommended. If the houses in the area where you are going to build are not a slab on grade type, do not be the first to try it. Usually, the local builder knows if the water table is too high for slab on grade floors.

If you are going to use a slab on grade system, I recommend a minimum of five-inch 4,000-PSI concrete slab with a six-inch wire-reinforcing grid with 8-gauge wire. Also, the toe footing around the perimeter would be twenty-four inches deep by twelve inches wide with two #5 rebar continuous in the toe.

If the floors are wood construction, be sure they are strong enough so that they do not bounce or sag. Squeaking is the result of wood moving against wood. So if the wood pieces are nailed, glued, or screwed properly, the floor will not squeak. Nails, glue, and screws are inexpensive, so use plenty of them on the floors, especially from the plywood to the framing. Also take into consideration the use of the room and the amount of the weight the floor will have to hold up. Rooms with a waterbed, pool table, library of books, or a dance floor need to have stronger floors than the powder room or a bedroom with a normal bed.

Wood floors on the ground floor over a crawl space are easy to make strong enough. The pier spacing should be around eight feet on center each way. The upper-level floors can become tricky, especially if the spans become long and heavy weights are on them.

Most wood floors consist of floor joists in the range of two-by-tens and two-by-twelves spaced at twelve and sixteen inches on center and not exceeding sixteen feet in spans. If deflections or strength are a concern, say from tile finish floors, the floor joists may double. A three-quarter-inch tong and groove plywood sub floor is usually installed on top of these floor joists. This plywood is glued and nailed, usually with 8cc nails six inches on center. The finish floor is usually installed next. This finish floor could be cement board with stone or tile, more wood and then carpet, just carpet, or a hardwood like maple or oak, or one of those exotic woods from the rainforest like mahogany or teak. Once you have seen one of those mahogany or teak floors installed, or better yet a mahogany sailboat or fine furniture, you know God made those trees to be lumber for artwork at a site-specific house.

I never could figure out why the TV programs show the logging trucks hauling out those millions of board feet of timber on logging roads that always go by the villages with the huts with dirt floors. It's a heartache, and I always yell at the TV, telling those dummies to cut down a tree and build a hut with a wood floor. I promise you, the tree will grow back. My wife tells me they can't hear me, so who's dumber, like she's pulling for the guy with a dirt floor even though you can eat off her floors. I say to her, "If you cut a tree down in the forest, and no one hears it fall, does it make a sound?" Then she forgets to put the butter and salt in my grits just the way she does to rude environmentalists.

I think hardwood floors with inlays and such, especially installed by a master carpenter, are a work of art but difficult and expensive to construct. Normal hardwood floors offer the same warmth as the fancy hardwood and are easy to install and relatively inexpensive.

For floors on the ground floor of a house, concrete floors with a tile or stone finish are relatively simple, and unless you use stone shipped in from Italy, they're inexpensive to construct. These concrete and stone or tile floors are used all over the world and have been throughout most of history. If you think they would be too cold, put a heavy rug on them.

Whichever floors you decide on, remember that the fundamental objective is to provide a stage to carry the inhabitants and their possessions. If all you have is a rock for a chair, then dirt works fine.

Chapter 17

Interior Trim and Cabinets

Kitchen cabinets with interior trim

I think everyone knows what cabinets are and that they are required in the kitchen, bathrooms, and laundry room. They are also helpful wherever there's a water fixture or a need for storage. Trim and cabinets go together, so I shall elucidate what trim means to me first.

Trim

By interior trim, I mean the molding that's used around the stairs, floors, cabinets, bookshelves, doors, windows, walls, ceilings, and anywhere else you want to use it. While trim is essential around door and window jambs, it's usually for decorations and appearances most other places.

Words that I hear used to describe trim, such as heavy or rich, do not explain the skill and true craftsmanship needed by a master carpenter to install it properly. While heavy or rich are words used by real estate salespersons to describe the amount or quality of the finish of the trim, I think words like complex, detailed, exact, and skilled more accurately describe trim work and cabinetwork. If you ever get the chance to just sit and watch for a short time while the trim is being installed at the ceiling-wall intersection or on stair rail or cabinet, you'll understand why trim takes so much time, and you'll appreciate the beauty of properly mitered joints. Most carpenters can butcher up some pretty wood and come close with the joints in double beveled miters, but master carpenters understand and can calculate to decimals of degrees, with their hand tools, the advanced geometry involved with properly installed trim. It is essential that trim or stained or varnished cabinets have exact joints with no gaps. Therein lies the rub, or I should say gap.

Wood shrinks with time. Even the finest made cabinets, furniture, and trim, unless kept in a controlled humidity environment, will shrink and the joints will open up. This will usually take years or decades, but it depends on the original moisture content of the wood and the ambient moisture content of the environment the wood is used in. Wood will eventually assume a condition of equilibrium with its environment. For example, wood begins to rot at above 19 percent moisture content; kiln dried wood is usually below 13 percent moisture content; and 9 percent is around the average humidity in a house. However, some people like very low humidity, and the wood shrinks so much that it actually makes noises. I once inspected a house with beautiful oak floors and stained cabinets and trim. The house was heated with wood stoves. The trim in the areas around these stoves did not stand a chance, and as the floors shrank, the joints would make a loud pop when the varnish over the joints popped open. The old bucket of water on top of the wood stove helped a lot, but the damage was done.

Trim is usually made of wood, but there are some trims made of composite material and plastic, which are becoming more and more in vogue. Most trim is painted, stained, or varnished. Stained and varnished trim require a more skilled carpenter than painted trim. With painted trim, the joints can be caulked, making it difficult to tell if the joint was mitered precisely. With trim that is not painted, this is extremely important. There is nothing uglier than open or poor joints in nice, clear wood trim. If you're going to use trim that's not painted, you have to use the best grade of wood in the longest pieces. The wood will be exposed, so any defects in the wood will show after it's installed. The longer the pieces, the fewer the joints, so you try to go from corner to corner with one piece of unpainted trim.

Painted trim usually will come in random lengths and be finger spliced together in the factory. Once it's painted, you should not see the finger joints. Trim usually comes in lengths of sixteen feet or less. If you have a room that's longer than that, there will be splices in the runs of trim. You can have trim made especially for you. You will need to locate a trim manufacturer and discuss the different styles of trim they make.

Trim around doors and windows should always be made in one piece. If your carpenter is using multiple pieces down the side of a door or window jamb, he's creating more work for himself, and you probably wouldn't want him as a son-in-law. Trim work is necessary around doors and windows and intersections of walls and floors to dress out and close the joints at those locations. The type and style of trim is up to the homeowner. You can use the minimum, simply a piece of lumber that's square on four sides, or you can have routed lumber with smooth, curved faces, or you can use multiple layers of various shapes. Some people get carried away with the amount of trim they use; they think you can't have enough. Crown molding is what I call the trim at the wall and ceiling intersection. Sometimes this joint is simply closed up with the Sheetrock and becomes a nice, neat square corner. Sometimes this joint is filled up with enough trim to build a battleship. It depends on what you like.

I think the trim should be coordinated with all the pieces of trim in the room being considered. Using narrow base trim at the floor intersection and then massive wide trim at the ceiling seems out of balance to me. Using well-coordinated trim that flows from the floor, up the window and doorjambs, and into the ceiling is just plain warm and comforting. I don't see the need to use a lot of trim in closets, pantries, storage rooms, and laundry rooms. Trim work is an expensive item in your house and can become very expensive if you use multiple layers with specially cut trim. A trip to the local lumber supplier is all it will take to see what's available in standard-type painted and unpainted trim. Most suppliers also have a selection of special run trim for those who want it. If you want one-of-a-kind of trim, you will need to talk to a company that makes trim.

Stair trim is a different monster altogether. Not only does the exacting homeowner get to see the joint work, they get to feel it too. There's nothing better than a stair handrail that flows and feels really smooth, and there's nothing worse than a rail that pinches the fingers or has rough spots. There's a whole industry involved with stairs and the trim associated with them. The amount of different kinds of stairs and rails and pickets that's already standard and published is one thing. Then there are the custom stairs for those who need the refinement and have the desire to torment the poor old master carpenter. As for me, most stairs and rails are pretty, unless they're so fragile you are afraid to touch them. Stair rails are there to help you and sometimes to prevent you from falling. They must be structurally sound. Most codes say they must support a load of fifty pounds per linear foot in any direction or a 200-pound concentrated load in any direction. That's usually enough, but I don't think they should move when you barely touch them with all 300 pounds of aunt Dixie, who just had the living daylights scared out of her at the top of the stairs by her favorite nephew who will never do that *Home Alone* trick again. Strong, solid stair rails are a good indication that the builder knows what he's doing.

One other thing about stair rails and the building codes is the use of pickets. Most codes require the pickets to be close enough together that a four-inch diameter sphere (ball) cannot be passed between them. There are even some inspectors that carry a ball around and try to stick it through the pickets. These guys bug me, and I would like to stick a picket in their sphere. When asked what the intent of the code is regarding this requirement, they usually, seriously respond with something like an infant cannot get its head stuck in the pickets. I personally think you should be able to install your pickets any way you want, or not even use them and just have rails if you like, especially if you do not have infants in your house. However, I can see the code writers' point on this. So if you catch a parent letting its infant get near the stairs, just tell them, "It's okay, your pickets meet the code—and so do the electric wall outlets for that matter." The point in all of this is that stairs can be somewhat of a hazard if not used correctly, and the trim around them should not only be pretty but functional. No one should play or be allowed to play on the stairs or with wall outlets. All the codes ever written cannot fix stupid, and the code writers should stop trying to do just that, or pretty soon there will be codes that read: *The following materials shall be considered specifically hazardous and cannot be used in human consumption. Nails, glass, asphalt shingles ...* (think of Alvin saying, "I wonder how Tony will like the taste of this glue on his corn beef and rye."). I think all that needs to be done with regard to residential construction and the codes is to not allow any three-year-olds, both mentally and physically, to build houses. Instead of getting a building permit, you would get an IQ test. There could be questions like "Do you think you are going to make a profit on this house?" Then again, I hear builders say all the time, "You got to be crazy to be in this business." Maybe a few codes isn't all that bad.

The cost of trim work is totally dependent upon the amount and the styles. Specially carved cherry wood trim does not cost the same as your standard painted spec house trim.

Cabinets

While you're at the lumber supplier, take a look at the cabinets. Most suppliers have a few brands of premade cabinets to choose from. Premade cabinets are sort of misleading. The cabinet manufacturers have standard size cabinets that they make. These cabinets have drawers or shelves and all types of Lazy Susans and are usually made from six inches to thirty-six inches in width and standard heights of thirty-six inches for base or wall-mounted cabinets. They are modules that you put together. They use thin fill strips if the length of the modules do not match exactly with the length of the wall the cabinets are going on. The quality of these cabinets ranges from poor to excellent. The building supplier will usually have someone who will help you put together the cabinet package for the space you have. Some people like to have their cabinets made specifically for the room they will be in. If that's the case, a cabinetmaker will come out and measure the room and build the cabinets to fit exactly in the space.

Either way you go, you have to decide on painted or not, the type of wood, and all of the gizmos that are available as inserts in the cabinets. You have to decide if you want shelves and how many, or drawers and how deep or high. You have to decide on the hardware you will need for the cabinets. Do you want handles or pull knobs, and what style? Do you want concealed or exposed hinges? Do you want drawer glides that are self-closing? The list goes on and on. There is a selection of ingenious things that you can stuff your cabinets full with that you have to decide on. Most housewives who cook already know about these things. The next time you take your wife shopping at the hardware store, leave her in the kitchen cabinet area while you're looking at the power tools; she won't be bored.

If you use a cabinetmaker to custom make your cabinets, they probably will take measurements and then make the cabinets at their shop and bring them to your house and install them. The cabinets will then have to be finished with paint or varnish, and that's covered under painting. If you select cabinets from a building supplier, they usually will come pre-finished. Whether you go with a cabinetmaker or premade cabinets, you need to be very specific about what you want. You need to have a drawing or sketch made of the elevation of the cabinets, showing where the drawers are and what size, where the shelves are and what size, where the gizmos are, and if the doors have glass in them or any type of fancy carvings or trim.

These drawings need to show where the ovens, stoves, refrigerators, and all appliances go with their required utilities and how they fit into the cabinets. If you know what appliances you're going to use, you can get the cut sheets on them that show all of this information. There's nothing exciting about having the cabinets in place and finished, and then the appliances don't fit. The appliances will all need electricity; some are hardwired with a dedicated circuit, and some just plug in. Some will need water or gas, and some will need to be exhausted to the outside. All of this is concealed inside the cabinets. This may require a drawer to be shorter than the rest of the drawers or an access panel to get to the electric box. Also, the switches to turn on these appliances, such as the garbage disposal and under-counter or in-cabinet lights, need to be located.

That's about all you need to get your cabinets right. I think the best way to do this is to look in magazines and tear out the pictures of the way you want your cabinets and appliances to look. Then give them to the cabinet people and let them give you sketches of what they're going to do. Without those sketches, you'll be relying entirely on the memory of everyone involved. The more detailed the cabinet plans are, the less memory is required, so insist that the cabinet people provide complete plans of what you're going to buy. That surprised look of a disappointed housewife is not going to convince a cabinetmaker he made it wrong.

Cabinets not only have to be considered for the kitchen but also for the powder room, bathrooms, vanity areas, laundry rooms, and wherever else you want them. The same things you have to decide in the kitchen, you have to decide in those rooms, just without the kitchen appliances. You do have to consider the plumbing for sinks and bathroom accessories. You may think that there are not a lot of bathroom accessories, but think again. There are robe hooks, towel bars, towel rings, soap dishes, soap dispensers, toothbrush holders, medicine cabinets, mirrors, paper towel dispensers, hand driers, toilet paper holders, and a variety of female instruments that need a storage place.

Some rooms in your house may need fine cabinetry and trim. The classic study usually has stained wood paneling and built-in bookcases and matching desk and credenza. This requires the work of a master carpenter. There's no such thing as a young master anything to me. So if you're going to have fine cabinetry, find a seasoned carpenter, ask to see his work, and then go check it out. The real pros are very proud of their creations and would gladly show it to you. Be warned, these guys are sensitive and consider their work as art, and you know how peculiar some artists are. Let's just say, when it comes to their trade, most master craftsmen have a strong quest for perfection and are not impatient, which is exactly what you need in trim work and cabinets.

Cabinets are both pretty and functional. They tend to range from $120 to $200 per foot in 2008 prices. These prices do not include glass for the doors, painting or staining, hardware, or countertops. The prices usually include installation and hinges.

Varnished wood starts out light and then turns darker with age.

For trim work that's stained or coated with a clear varnish, the wood gets darker over the years. Even if you use a light-colored wood with clear varnish, as the years pass, the wood will darken on its own. The wood in the above picture is white pine with a clear varnish, and after fifty years, it has turned dark. With varnished wood, if it turns to a color you don't like, you can always paint it.

Chapter 18

Paint, Finishes, and the Punch List

I have always thought that painting provides more bang for the buck than any other trade in the housing industry does. Painting transforms plain Sheetrock into a dramatic lush backdrop for your space. Everyone knows generally what painting is all about, and most everyone has painted a room or two at some point. That being the case (and this not being a technical type of book), I'm just going to hit the general points of painting.

By painting, I mean the covering, with the many fluid materials used as thin coatings, on various solid materials like Sheetrock, wood, and masonry. For the purposes of this book, paint includes varnish, stain, lacquer, enamel, sealer, water based, oil based, resins, latex, white wash, linseed oil, tong oil, China oil, epoxy, fish oil, red lead, zinc oxide, inorganic, organic, titanium white, aluminum fine flake, alkyd, synthetic, plastic, glazes, transparent liquids, and the list increases every year.

One very important thing: no matter what kind of paint you decide on, do not under any circumstances eat it. For centuries, lead has been an additive in paint. It's very beneficial in helping paint stick to the surface it's applied to and in preventing the paint from peeling. There has been a big to-do in the last few years about eating paint and getting lead poison. I have read about this, but I have never met anyone who has ever even met anyone that has known anyone this has happened to. I guess most of the people I know have not developed a taste for paint and watch their children closely enough so that they do not eat paint. They make sure the babies have something to suck or chew on besides the edges of a crib or chair. Anyway, they took the lead out of paint to keep us from eating paint and killing ourselves. Now paint is not as durable as it used to be, and it peels quicker than in the old days. I'm still glad they put the warning on the paint cans, "not for human consumption," just in case someone mistakes the paint can for a gallon of milk during a midnight feeding. You know, "Here, junior, some fresh milk to go with those paint chips on your crib," or just in case someone said, "I wonder how this glass of paint will taste with these Oreos."

Usually in the spring, the home improvement stores will offer their brand-new, one coat, anywhere, anytime, rain or shine, self-applying, interior, exterior, self-cleaning, double lifetime warranty, match any color, lead-free, deluxe paint line. On sale if you move fast. I guess they figure cabin fever has rendered the men in the house brain dead, and the women have never before seen a color that enhances everything they own. In other words, your life is not worth living if you don't spend an hour changing the color of your dining room. Usually, the ads show some glamorous lady dressed in the latest fashion. She just got her hair and nails done, is holding a Louis IX pocketbook, is painting the dining room with this magic paint, and everything looks magnificent—and she did it all in between the time she was changing the kids' diapers. Easy, easy, easy; everybody knows there ain't nothing to it.

I think the reason most people think this, or do not give painters their due, is because most good painters wear white painter's clothes and make their employees wear them too. Everyone knows what a painter looks like. So when you see a painter buying a beer after work, you know he's a painter by his clothes—thus the belief that painters are prolific drinkers. I can assure you, they are no different from people in any of the other trades; you just don't know what people in the other trades look like. I think painters wear white clothes because most paints were white in the old days. Painters take pride in not getting paint on themselves, and white on white makes sense that way. Today, you will see dabs of different color paints on the whites, and you know the person is a painter. If you see a whole bunch of dabs, you know he's an inexperienced painter. Have mercy on him; they have been playing painter's tricks on him all day—thus the paint all over his new whites.

One such trick is when a painter puts his bucket and brush down for a break. Prior to setting down the bucket, the painter will dress up the paint runs on the bucket and sides of the brush. Then he will set the brush down in the bucket if the paint is not too deep, or he will set the brush on top of the bucket. All nice and clean and ready to start again after his break.

One of his good friends will take his brush and paint the underneath side of the handle with a nice thick coat and set it back right where it was. The time bell rings, and the experienced painters pick up their brushes with two fingers to check for this old trick. The inexperienced painter, his mind full of his ideas for the maritime trade agreements between Kansas and the defunct USSR, grabs his brush with his whole hand. At this time, it becomes obvious why no one knows who painted the backside of his brush. Now instead of helping the president with the trade agreements, he has to concentrate on revenge or where the next moron's attack will come from. In reality, he knows he'll have to wait until the rookie with the new whites arrives all fresh and ready and not a drop of paint on them, claiming, "Heck yeah, I'm a painter."

Other finishes, besides paint, are things like wallpaper, mirrored walls, textured walls, and so on. Wallpaper requires the same type of surface preparation as painting, and the wall should get a primer coat of paint before the wallpaper goes on. I personally do not like wallpaper because you cannot paint it when the color gets old and tired and you need a color that lives like pastel chartreuse. However, wallpaper is pretty interesting, and sometimes you cannot tell which is up or down with the pattern. You usually don't find out until the room is finished and your sister-in-law says it's upside down, and you were helping her hang it for free. Some wallpaper is made out of vinyl, and they say it's useful when you have to scrub the walls. So if your children have a lot of food fights at the kitchen table, you might want to consider vinyl wallpaper in the kitchen. Most paint stores sell wallpaper, and most painters say they can hang paper, too. So if you like wallpaper, as with paint, there seems like an endless supply to choose from.

One good thing is they have not found any lead in wallpaper, yet, and some people say you can eat the glue. I'll stick with paint even though the dice could be loaded.

Painting can be broken into four phases: selecting the painter, preparation for paint, interior painting, and exterior painting. These are in the order of importance to me.

Selecting the Painter

Hire a paint contractor who has a minimum of ten years of experience and a permanent place of business. This paint contractor should have all required licenses, permits, insurances, and workers' compensation requirements in order. He should have recommendations from previously completed projects and especially from the paint manufacturer for the type of paint you're going to use. If the paint colors have not already been selected, he should be able to give you paint chips or color brochures to help in the selection. You should make a trip to the paint store that the painter recommends and check out his relationship with them. If you wish, the painter should be able to assist with the colors of paint you choose. He also should paint some sample colors on the walls to be sure the colors are the right ones.

He should be able to tell you how many men he is going to use, when the men will arrive on site each day, and when they will leave. He should ask about where he is to clean up. This is an important point, and the location should be somewhere away from the house where paint slopped on the ground will not bother anything and is out of sight. He should be able to tell you how long the job will take, including preparations and drying time.

He should be able to tell you how much paint he will need. Be careful with the painter specifying the number of coats he will use. Some paints are thicker than others, and the number of coats has very little to do with the actual thickness of the paint coat. There are devices that can tell you exactly how thick the paint coat is. I suggest that you rely on the paint manufacturer's written recommendations for paint thickness and number of coats. Also, the paint should be applied until the paint looks rich and lush; then you have enough. You don't care how many coats it takes.

He should be able to tell you how much the job will cost. I would expect him to discuss paying for the material cost, such as the paint, sandpaper, cleanup fluids, and other things, once the material is delivered on site. His price should be a guaranteed maximum price unless you change something. Then a change order should be agreed upon before the painter starts work on the change. The original price with the change order should be agreed upon prior to doing the new work. Change orders do not necessarily mean an add-on to the painter's price. Let's say you decided to tile some walls instead of painting them. You should know how much you are going to pay and when the payments are due. Some painters like to be paid weekly or biweekly; it's up to you and the painter to work that out. I recommend holding 10 percent of every request for payment and the entire last payment until the job is finished, including the punch list items. How much you hold should be agreed upon before the painter begins work.

What all this boils down to is this: Painting should be a combination of skill and art. Hire a painter who considers the painting of your house as the creation of one of his masterpieces. Hire someone you like and who is honest and agree upon a fair price.

Preparation for Painting

Now that you have selected the painter, he should begin the preparation phase for the painting of your house. The preparation to paint is the real work in painting. Depending on the material you are painting, the quality of the carpenter installing the wood trim, and other items to be painted, the preparation can take as much time as the painting itself.

To begin, for interior work, all the other trades' work should be completed so that no one else is working in the house but the painters. This especially includes the trim carpenters and all the trim work around the cabinets, doors, windows, stairways, and everything that does not move and gets painted. The house should be well lit with the permanent lights or with movable temporary lights. The candlepower of these lights should be the same brightness as when the permanent lights will be on. If the painter cannot see what he's doing, he cannot be expected to do his best work. So be forewarned: if the painter has to paint in the dark, it's not the same as a blind golfer playing at night.

The house should be vacuumed clean of all sawdust, regular dust, and all debris that winds up in the floor of a house under construction. All nail and screw holes need to be filled with wood putty, and all joints need to be caulked. If certain wood trim pieces or cabinets and doors are to be stained, then the preparation becomes even more tedious. The wood putty must match the wood, and the joints cannot be caulked, so they have to be tight to begin with. Staining is much more time consuming and difficult than painting. After all the holes and joints are addressed, everything needs to be sanded as smooth as a baby's bottom and then cleaned and dusted off. Whatever should not get paint on it should be taped, removed, or covered up, so that paint cannot land on it.

For exterior work, the preparation is similar to the interior preparation; there just is not as much trim work to cut around. Caulking joints and filling nail holes still should be done. Sanding and dusting off are required, but not as thoroughly as with the interior work.

Once the prep work is completed, it should be inspected for any missed holes or joints, but more importantly, the surface of the walls, cabinets, doors, and trim should be felt with your hands to be sure they're smooth to the touch. There is nothing worse than sliding your hand down a stair rail and feeling grit or particles on the smooth surface. Once the prep work is completed, the house should be vacuumed again.

Interior and Exterior Painting

Let the painting commence. The initial coat of paint that is applied on the raw surfaces is usually called the primer, sealer, sanding sealer, and so on. What it means is that this first coat is a little thinner than regular paint so that it will penetrate deeper into the surfaces. After this coat dries, it is sanded and dusted off, and the finish coats of paint are applied. The finish coats of paint will be the ones where the color and sheen are selected. The color is something only you can pick. The sheen has to do with whether the paint is flat or glossy. Most people use water-based flat paint for the walls and oil-based semi-gloss for the trim. Paint can be applied in many ways. Spraying, rolling, and brushing are the typical ways houses are painted. All of the methods will work for getting the right amount of the right color and the right type of the right paint on the right part of the right house. After all that, the color probably would be pastel chartreuse.

Once the painting is completed and dried, then all of the things that were taken down to make the painting easier must be put back in place. Be sure they are put back in place correctly. The doors should have been numbered so that the door that was fit to its original opening goes back in that opening. All the electrical plates and light fixtures go back up.

Painting the exterior of the house is totally independent from the interior. The outside can be painted anytime the exterior of the house is ready. The preparation is the same. The only major difference is the weather. Paint should be applied per the manufacturer's written recommendations. Usually, the manufacturer wants the weather to be at least forty-five degrees and rising so that the paint does not freeze. It's just common sense; do not paint in the rain and things like that.

So one more time, paint the Sheetrock with flat, water-based latex and the trim with semi-gloss oil-based enamel and use as many coats as it takes to make the paint look rich.

The Punch List

Punch lists are never fun. To begin with, it's someone's job to find everything the painter did wrong and now should fix. It's much easier to go through and point out everything that's right, and that should be a lot more than what's on the punch list. The owner should get the opportunity to walk through the house and do a punch list only one time. The punch list should be done when everyone thinks they're finished, especially the painter. Sometimes the carpet will go in after the original punch list, and if this happens, the owner gets to do another list after the carpet installation.

The punch list should be done under the same light as the house was painted in. The person doing the punch list should stand at least five feet from the surface being inspected. I recommend that little, round, orange stickers be used to locate and identify the areas in question. A number is written on the sticker and on a corresponding sheet of paper describing the punch item. For example: Item 15, paint run in wall. There should be a space on the sheet of paper, with the description of the punch item, for the initials of the person who corrected the punch item and the date of when it was done. If there is not a sticker, the person most likely will not find the run, and this can create some confusion if the item was marked done. Again, the punch list should only be done once but done thoroughly and completely with the homeowner and someone responsible for the work.

After the painter is through, he probably will offer to give you the leftover paint to touch up with after a few months. Unless you just want to have several cans of opened and unopened paint sitting around your house, tell him thanks but no thanks. He should clean up all his waste and supplies himself and leave your house freshly painted.

Chapter 19

Glass, Smoke, and Mirrors

Mirrored wall in bathroom

Have you ever been in a barbershop where they have a plate glass mirror in front of you and one in back of you? When you look just right into the mirrors, it seems that your reflection goes on forever. Or, have you been to a carnival with a glass fun house and gotten lost or looked in those concave and convex mirrors that make you look odd? Have you ever started a fire with a magnifying glass or gotten even with fire ants coming out of a fire ant hill? Be careful with that one.

I once bet a college ROTC student from New Jersey, who worked for me part time, twenty dollars that he couldn't stand on a fire ant hill for fifteen seconds. He had never seen a fire ant hill and didn't know why they call them fire ants. On a hot summer day, he, two of his buddies, and I had been running a topo on a piece of property that had fire ant hills all over it. He was wearing army boots that came up above his ankles, short pants, and a T-shirt. We picked out a nice big twelve-inch tall one for him; his two buddies knew what fire ants were. Today, when I run into those two guys, the three of us still laugh about how quickly the city boy learned about intentionally stepping on a fire ant hill. Not only did he get the hell bit out of him, but he lost twenty dollars. They told me he got sick from all that ant poison he took in from those bites. We took the magnifying glass off a compass and showed him how to incinerate the ants as they came out of a hole in the mound. I think it helped him recover from the ridicule his ROTC buddies gave him, especially when he told them how he got even with the little bastards (his words) with the magnifying glass and then went around at the end of the day and chopped all the hills he could find in half with the bush axe. Now that I think about it, I don't think that city boy had ever played with a magnifying glass or seen a bush axe. Prisms are another cool use of glass. Every house needs glass things to entertain certain curious grownup kids. Most acids and gases, with the exception of hydrofluoric acid, will not affect glass.

Glass and mirrors always add a type of mysterious interest to any room. They can also add an entertaining jewel or a useful and practical function. Have you ever looked at a mirror and wondered if it's a one-way mirror and there's someone looking right back at you? If you've ever watched *Law and Order*, the cops always stand behind the one-way mirror and study the suspect as if the one-way mirror gives them more insight than standing face-to-face. There could be some truth to that. There should be plenty of mirrors placed in strategic places in all houses. A dangerous intersection in a hall needs a mirror so you can see who's about to run into you. You can tell the young men taking your daughter out that some of the mirrors in the house are one-way. All bathrooms need plenty of mirrors. Mirroring one whole wall in a room can really confuse some people. Animals wonder what's what when they see themselves in a mirror. You can reflect natural light from the sun to some point in your house, just like the Egyptians used mirrors to reflect light into the pyramids.

Glass walls or fixed glass windows are useful to accent something or to open up an area. Enclosing a helix stair in a glass stair shaft is cool. Having a fixed glass window between two rooms allows visual access to the room and keeps the noise in. Large exterior walls of glass aren't typical in residential construction like they are in commercial construction. In commercial construction, the whole front of a store is usually glass. This type of glass framing is called storefront and is made mostly of aluminum mullions around two to four feet wide and from floor to ceiling in height. The glass is usually insulated and the structural type that's hard to break.

When you use glass or mirrors around areas where you could fall into them, they have to be the safety glass type that doesn't shatter everywhere when it breaks. This type of glass has a thin layer of clear plastic between layers of glass. The plastic holds it together if it breaks. If you think you need it, they make bulletproof glass and glass you can walk on.

Mirrors and glass can be reasonably priced or out-of-this-world priced. It depends on what you do to the glass. The raw materials for glass (sand, limestone, soda ash, sodium sulfate, and some alumina) are inexpensive. All these materials and some others are heated to around 3000°F and then made into different shapes and colors with different processes. After the glass returns to the solid state, it will continue to be processed, such as beveled glass panes or etched glass. How much work is done to the glass determines how much it costs.

Extra special care and tools are needed to handle glass safely. I think it's best to let the glass company install the glass and mirrors in the house. This eliminates the possibility of seven years of bad luck.

Chapter 20

Carpet

I separate carpet from floors because it's typically one of the last things to be installed in a house. Wood floors go in and then need to be trimmed out and/or finished. When carpet goes in, that's it. Once it's in, you can walk on it.

Carpet is sold by the square yard, which is three feet by three feet or nine square feet. People who don't understand carpet will figure the square feet in the rooms they want carpeted and then divide it by nine, and that's how many yards of carpet they think they should pay for. If all the rooms worked out to be whole yard numbers like nine-by-nine or fifteen-by-fifteen or twenty-four-by-twenty-four, that would be true. In reality, most rooms are some odd number like twelve feet nine inches by thirteen feet. You would have to buy a piece of carpet fifteen feet wide for that room. That's what you have to understand when you figure out how much carpet costs.

Like everything else, carpet comes in different qualities with corresponding prices. All carpet should come with a foam underlayment or mat. This gives the carpet the soft comfortable feeling. This mat comes in different qualities also. Some people think it's better to get a good quality mat and average carpet than the other way around. I think you just settle on an installed price per square yard and then fit the carpet and mat into that price. I recommend that you purchase the stuff they spray on the carpet to keep fluids from soaking into the fibers. As people with kids and pets already know, this stuff works well for liquids; however, it does not work at all for lit cigarettes. I just threw that in because there are only a few things that make the lady of the house angrier than a cig burn on the carpet.

At today's prices, a good quality carpet and mat would be around $35 per square yard installed. I heard the carpet in the oval office of the White House costs $750 per square yard installed and is replaced every time there's a new president. But then, the White House isn't your average house. The president isn't paying for it, we are; so in a sense, we've all bought some very expensive carpet at one time or another. When the carpet salesman tries to sell you the expensive stuff, tell him that it's in your other house.

Chapter 21

Appliances and Furnishings

My friend and her sink. When you treat women well
with new appliances, they'll love you forever.

In today's house, the appliances are not limited to the kitchen, although
those are the ones most people think about. Appliances are typically not
moved around the house too much. While you're on the couch watching
the crucial play in a game, you don't often hear, "Honey, how do you think

the oven will look over here by the sink?" or, "I think it's time to rearrange the kitchen." Appliances typically stay in one place because of the special electrical and utility lines they require. People usually don't run 220-volt outlets to every wall just in case you want to see how the oven looks in different places.

So what are appliances? How about a safe, audio, video, barbeque, game tables, exercise machines, printers, plotters, office equipment, ice machines, water fountains, beverage centers, wine centers, ovens, stoves, refrigerators, freezers, microwaves, fireplaces, lights, trash compactors and recycling centers, washers, dryers, scales, tools, children's toys, copying machines, special work centers, medical, and don't forget the appliances for pets. Think of how much patience you need after you rearrange the kitchen and laundry room and then hear, "I think it looked better the way it was." Now, if you live in some parts of the South, you've got to put that heavy, old washing machine back on the front porch by the freezer.

I consider furnishings to be the movable furniture like chairs, tables, beds, dressers, sofas, paintings, and all the things both antique and modern that clutter up the house. That's not counting the rented mini-warehouse where everybody's stuff that doesn't fit in the house goes—things you just can't live without like the futon your son used in college that smells like it was the perfect place to vomit. I'm not talking about firearms and power tools and the essential things like that—you know, the things you just like to play with while you're drinking. Those things require prominent places in your house. There is nothing better than a double barrel shotgun over the fireplace.

All the locations in your house for all of the above items, and the ones you can think of, must be addressed during the planning stages of your house. These items should be shown on a floor plan drawn specifically for them. If they're not dimensionally worked out on the floor plans prior to building the house, I guarantee they will not work out when the house is finished. The law of physics that says you can't rearrange matter and decrease the volume is true. What that means, in common sense, is that no matter how many times you rearrange the room, the furniture will not get smaller and the room will not get bigger. If your common sense isn't working, your sense of humor better be when the stuff doesn't fit. Please layout all the furniture and appliances you're going to have in your house to the correct scale on the floor plan before you start to build.

If you're working with a good architect or designer, that should be one of the first things that's discussed. Some people think the house is just to keep the rain off your things, but we know it's a little more than that.

Most people have some idea of how much appliances and furniture cost. Most stores that sell these items have a website that gives you the cost information you would need.

Modern kitchen appliances don't seem to have that warm, romantic touch like the ones of yesteryear.

Chapter 22

Landscaping

Landscaping always increases curb appeal. Just don't park on the daisies.

Landscaping is a little outside the scope of this book; however, because a new house sitting on a bare lot that's just gone through construction looks bad, I am going to lightly touch on it.

My friends in the real estate business would say a house with no landscaping has horrible curb appeal, and to me, the landscaping is the first impression. The house may be perfect, but it won't look perfect or finished until the outside is dressed up. The more dressed up, the better the first impression. Although a good landscape contractor can come in and roll out grass, plant bushes and trees, and you'll have a finished look, landscaping is more of a long-term project. If you love to work in the yard, you most likely should hire a landscape architect to assist you with a general overall plan. If you're going to have lights in your yard, which I think is cool, and jewel type items like that, you should use a landscape architect to work out a really detailed plan. This plan would incorporate the climate you live in and the vegetation that's indigenous to your area.

If you prefer things *au naturel*, then let nature take its course. Of course, there are many options between these two sides of the spectrum, and you have to decide what's best for you and how much you want to invest in your yard at this time.

There are a few items that are the same for all houses. After the house is completed, all of the construction debris should be hauled away. That does not mean dig a hole and bury it onsite. The site should be finished graded with small tractors and hand tools and left by the house builder in a neat, organized manner ready for landscaping. Most sidewalks and driveways are built by the contractor that builds the house. Driveways are usually no more than a hundred feet long; after that, it should be considered a road. If your driveway isn't just leading to the garage, but is curving around into a type of ride that you experience as you approach the entrance to your house, you definitely need a landscape architect.

If you decide to install an irrigation system, be sure the sprinkler heads aren't aimed at the house and that they don't saturate the house foundations every time they come on. If the sprinkler heads soak the soil around the foundations, the dirt will turn into mud and the house will settle. One other thing about sprinkler heads is that they always seem to be right by the driveway or road, and every time you run off the edge of the driveway or park on the curb, you smash one of these heads. I recommend that you put these heads far enough away from the driving paths so you don't have to worry about them getting run over. If you put these things where they can get run over, they will, and you won't know it until the system comes on, and then the water usually will shoot straight up in the air or somewhere that you definitely don't want wet.

It takes time and maintenance to make plants grow and is greatly dependent on the seasons of the year. If your house is finished in the winter, you probably should put off serious landscaping until the spring. The landscaper is going to tell you that he will guarantee his plants will live if they're maintained and watered. I guarantee a few of them are going to die no matter what you do, especially if you don't have a green thumb.

Be prepared to develop your landscaping over several years. Having a landscaped yard sets the stage for your house.

Unless the landscaping is minimal, such as rolling out some grass in the front yard and planting some bushes across the front of the house, the cost of it usually isn't included in the cost of the house. This item needs to be discussed with the homeowner and the contractor prior to finalizing the price of the work. Most homebuilders are not landscapers, but they usually know some and would prefer that you contract directly with the landscaper. If you contract separately with a landscaper, be sure he and the house builder communicate early on so that the painters don't clean their oil brushes right where you were going to plant a Chinese cherry tree. Also, the locations of the utility lines, such as water, sewer, gas, phone, cable, and electric, will need to be coordinated with the landscaper's plans. Cutting these lines at anytime is not fun, especially if you have not notified the proper authorities that you'll be digging in the area of these utilities.

By the way, everyone is required to notify the proper authorities any time they will be digging around utility lines. If you do not do this, you can and usually are fined by the authorities and called dirty names by the neighbors when their cable or water is temporally cut off. If you cut the electric or gas line, which are usually buried much deeper than the water, phone, or cable, and if you live, you will be fined and your neighbors might not visit you in the hospital. Always locate these utility lines on your property when they're installed. If you asked the surveyor who does your boundary line survey for the financial institutes, he will locate them on your plat.

Landscape costs are dependent on the amount of plants and grasses and how exotic the plants are. Landscapers will tell you how much attention, sun, and water each plant requires and if you have to do special things to them in the winter. There are many neat special effects that your landscaper can create, such as water bubbling out from a boulder and waterfalls and goldfish ponds and thing like that. All these things add to the cost. The one thing I think you should keep in mind is that your landscape plan should reflect how much work you like to do in the yard. My favorites are the plants that have the most color and require the least amount of maintenance. Sometimes having one of those plants that's shaped like Elvis or a couple of concrete statues isn't too bad either, unless it takes away from the flamingos.

Chapter 23

Cost and Scheduling

If you're going to build a house, you will need a thought-out set of design plans and an experienced residential contractor. Based on the plans, the contractor will develop an accurate detailed cost analysis and a realistic construction schedule. The more detailed and clear the plans are, the more accurate the construction cost and schedule will be. The cost analysis and schedule should tell you how much money you will be spending per month during construction. The finances you will need to build your house, including a contingency amount, should be in place before you start construction. This book will help with everything but the money. Your banker should be able to help you there.

I like to assign importance or cost to the different aspects or elements involved with a house. I like to know how much an item costs compared to the total cost of the house. The method I use to assign relative dollar value to each part of the total house price is in a general cost analysis. The general cost analysis is a synopsis of the detailed cost analysis, kind of like a short form of the detailed cost analysis.

A detailed cost analysis includes a description and cost for every single itty-bitty tiny item associated with the construction of the house. These detailed cost analyses are the result of an accurate takeoff of material and labor for everything involved with the construction of the house. If the contractor has done a detailed cost analysis, he can show it to you and explain which items he has combined under each line item in the general cost analysis. If he has not done a detailed cost analysis, don't trust the estimate for the cost of the house. A good contractor will have a detailed cost analysis, which he should be willing to give to you if you hire him to build your house, but only if you really want to know how much 16cc nails cost per pound, and were the heads on the right end, and did he use those nails on the right side of the house, and did those nails with the head on the other end go on the other side of the house, then you'll need the detailed cost analysis. Some people need that much detail and are willing to pay for it. However, I would stick with a general cost analysis with an explanation of what each line item covers.

The general cost analysis of the house does not include the cost of the land. The cost of the land and associated site work can be substantial and are usually a separate item involving the overall cost of the project. This may seem dumb because the owner is going to pay both bills; however, in order to assign importance to house items properly, just the house costs need to be analyzed. The house cost involves everything associated with the house within five feet of the house perimeter. The number of line items in the general cost analysis can vary to as few or as many as you like by combining several items into one. I like to keep a general breakdown to around forty line items. These will fit on one legal size sheet of paper. I like the general cost analysis line item to provide the total cost of each item, which includes material, labor, overhead, taxes, and everything involved with the item. Then, I like for it to be broken down as number of units or items and a total cost per installed unit or per square foot. Finally, I like to know how much it is in terms of a percentage of the total cost of the house. It gives you this kind of information: *Line item—carpet. There are fifty yards of carpet, it costs $35.00 per yard installed, the total cost of installed carpet is $2,000, and it is 1 percent of the total cost of the house.* From this general analysis, you can see by looking at one sheet of paper the dollar value or importance of each part of the house relative to another and to the total cost of the house. Sometimes it helps to see if you have placed too much importance on wallpaper and not enough on windows.

It's funny how cost seems to come up in everything we do. We always want to know what the real cost is with all the fine print and hidden things. I believe there are two costs in everything we buy. There's the initial cost, which we always like to be as low as possible. Then, there's the real cost or the life cycle cost. The house you're building also has two prices, the initial cost and life cycle cost. Sometimes we only have so much money and can only address the initial cost. However, it's usually best to look at the life cycle cost if you plan on staying in the house for life.

I hope I've covered the cost of the house throughout the book in enough detail for you to get an understanding of the overall price of the house. I also hope I've emphasized which elements of a house are the most important ones and when cost should not be the only thing considered.

On the following page is a typical detailed cost estimate. Across the top of the sheet should be a header that tells the name and location of the house and the total roofed square feet in the house.

This is not the only type of cost estimate; it just gives you an idea of how the cost of your house can be broken down.

NAME FOR HOUSE ESTIMATE
DATE
LOCATION OF HOUSE
ROOFED SQUARE FEET 3382

ITEM	UNITS	QUANTITY	MATERIAL COST	MATERIAL TOTAL	LABOR COST	LABOR TOTAL	SUB CONTRACTOR	TOTAL COST	ROOFED SF C(
GENERAL CONDITIONS	MONTH	9.00	$400.00	$3,600.00	$200.00	$1,800.00		$5,400.00	$1.60
SITE CLEARING	ACRE	3.5	$0.00	$0.00	$0.00	$0.00		$0.00	$0.00
ROUGH GRADING	ACRE	3.5	$0.00	$0.00	$500.00	$1,750.00		$1,750.00	$0.52
DRIVE WAY	SF	13200	$0.40	$5,280.00	$0.50	$6,600.00		$11,880.00	$3.51
UTILITY HOOK UP	1	1	$250.00	$250.00	$250.00	$250.00		$500.00	$0.15
WELL	FT	800	$3.00	$2,400.00	$9.00	$7,200.00		$9,600.00	$2.84
SEPTIC SYSTEM	FT	300	$2.00	$600.00	$8.00	$2,400.00		$3,000.00	$0.88
FINE GRADING	SF	4000	$0.30	$1,200.00	$0.13	$520.00		$1,720.00	$0.51
TERMITE TREATMENT	1	1		$0.00		$0.00	$300.00	$300.00	$0.09
HOUSE LAY OUT	SF	3382	$0.10	$338.20	$0.15	$507.30		$845.50	$0.25
HOUSE FND & SOG	YD	80	$157.00	$9,420.00	$63.00	$3,780.00		$13,200.00	$3.90
B PORCH FND & SOG	YD	8	$157.00	$1,256.00	$160.00	$1,280.00		$2,536.00	$0.75
HOUSE STEPS	YD	12	$157.00	$1,884.00	$160.00	$1,920.00		$3,804.00	$1.12
HOUSE ROUGH FRAMING	SF	3142	$12.50	$39,275.00	$5.00	$15,710.00		$54,985.00	$16.26
FIRE PLACE	1	1		$0.00		$0.00	$5,000.00	$5,000.00	$1.48
BACK PORCH FRAMING	SF	246	$11.50	$2,790.00	$6.00	$1,440.00		$4,200.00	$1.24
ROOFING & FLASHING	SQ	80	$60.00	$5,000.00	$75.00	$4,500.00		$7,500.00	$2.22
UPPER DECK FRAMING	SF	320	$9.30	$2,976.00	$4.00	$1,280.00		$4,256.00	$1.26
CORNICE & EXT. TRIM	LF	256	$6.00	$1,500.00	$2.00	$500.00		$2,000.00	$0.59
WINDOWS	EACH	20	$384.00	$7,680.00	$40.00	$800.00		$8,480.00	$2.51
EXTERIOR DOORS	EACH	5	$1,000.00	$5,000.00	$80.00	$400.00		$5,400.00	$1.60
SIDING	SF	3358	$2.70	$9,066.60	$1.00	$3,358.00		$12,424.60	$3.67
STAIR FRAMING	SF	84	$2.00	$168.00	$5.00	$420.00		$588.00	$0.17
PLUMBING	FIXTURE	25	$200.00	$5,000.00	$200.00	$5,000.00	$0.00	$10,000.00	$2.96
HVAC	1	1		$0.00		$0.00	$9,000.00	$9,000.00	$2.66
ELECTRICAL	1	1		$0.00		$0.00	$10,000.00	$10,000.00	$2.96
ROOF INSULATION	SF	3142	$0.21	$659.82	$0.21	$659.82		$1,319.64	$0.39
FLOOR INSULATION	SF	2020	$0.25	$505.00	$0.25	$505.00		$1,010.00	$0.30
EXT WALL INSULATION	SF	3840	$0.22	$805.20	$0.22	$805.20		$1,610.40	$0.48
SOUND INSULATION	SF	1500	$0.25	$375.00	$0.25	$375.00		$750.00	$0.22
SHEET ROCK	SF	12900	$0.30	$3,870.00	$0.50	$6,450.00		$10,320.00	$3.05
LIGHT FIXTURES	EACH	85	$60.00	$5,100.00	$15.00	$1,275.00		$6,375.00	$1.88
TILE WALLS & CEILINGS	SF	494	$4.00	$1,976.00	$4.00	$1,976.00		$3,952.00	$1.17
TILE FLOORS	SF	577	$4.00	$2,308.00	$4.00	$2,308.00		$4,616.00	$1.36
SHOWER TILE FLOORS	SF	36	$30.00	$1,080.00	$30.00	$1,080.00		$2,160.00	$0.64
INTERIOR STONE WORK	SF	130	$7.00	$910.00	$5.00	$650.00		$1,560.00	$0.46
HARD WOOD FLOORS	SF	1361	$3.00	$4,083.00	$1.00	$1,361.00		$5,444.00	$1.61
CABINETS & ISLAND	LF	65	$120.00	$7,800.00	$20.00	$1,300.00		$9,100.00	$2.69
INTERIOR DOORS	EACH	23	$150.00	$3,450.00	$25.00	$575.00		$4,025.00	$1.19
INTERIOR TRIM & STAIR	LF	4324	$1.10	$4,756.40	$0.50	$2,162.00		$6,918.40	$2.05
COUNTER TOPS	SF	130	$15.00	$1,950.00	$5.00	$650.00		$2,600.00	$0.77
PLUMBING FIXTURES	EACH	16	$238.00	$3,808.00	$0.00	$0.00		$3,808.00	$1.13
PLUMBING HARDWARE	EACH	16	$210.00	$3,360.00	$0.00	$0.00		$3,360.00	$0.99
INTERIOR PAINTING	SF	12900	$0.19	$2,451.00	$0.50	$6,450.00		$8,901.00	$2.63
EXTERIOR PAINTING	SF	3358	$0.13	$436.54	$0.50	$1,679.00		$2,115.54	$0.63
DOOR HARDWARE	EACH	22	$50.00	$1,100.00	$15.00	$330.00		$1,430.00	$0.42
MIRRORS	EACH	6	$200.00	$1,200.00	$20.00	$120.00		$1,320.00	$0.39
FINISH WOOD FLOORS	SF	1361	$0.20	$272.20	$0.80	$1,088.80		$1,361.00	$0.40
KITCHEN APPLIANCES	EACH	4	$1,350.00	$5,400.00	$20.00	$80.00		$5,480.00	$1.62
WASHER & DRYER	EACH	2	$1,000.00	$2,000.00	$20.00	$40.00		$2,040.00	$0.60
CARPET	SF	1368	$2.50	$3,420.00	$0.33	$451.44		$3,871.44	$1.14
CLEAN UP & PUNCH LIST	1	1		$0.00		$0.00	$500.00	$500.00	$0.15
EXTERIOR STONE WORK	SF	0	$7.00	$0.00	$5.00	$0.00		$0.00	$0.00
LANDSCAPING	1	1		$0.00		$0.00	$5,000.00	$5,000.00	$1.48
TOTALS				$165,729.96		$93,788.56	$29,800.00	$289,316.52	$85.55
MATERIAL TAXES				$11,601.10					
TOTAL COST				$177,331.06		$93,788.56	$29,800.00	$300,917.62	$88.98
OH AND PROFIT 10%								$30,091.76	$8.90
TOTAL CONSTRUCTION								$331,009.38	$97.87

Figure 9. Detailed cost estimate

Chapter 24
Warranty and Maintenance

Well made but neglected portion of a house

No matter how maintenance free you've made your house, it will still require weekly work, if nothing more than taking out the trash. Entropy, some say, is a doctrine of inevitable degeneration. In plain words, if you sweep the floor and leave the pile in the middle of the floor, it will eventually spread back out all over the floor. Your house eventually will turn into a mound of rubble. Check out the Roman Empire ruins. However, with proper maintenance your house will last for millenniums.

If you do not maintain your house, it will, quicker than you think, deteriorate. If you do not change the filters in the HVAC systems, they will break. If you do not address water in all locations in the house, it will have negative effects. Pipes leak. Caulking dries out. All things mechanical wear out and need replacing or repairs. Paint and shingles do not last forever. Wood shrinks and warps. Concrete cracks. Dust builds up everywhere. Bugs get everywhere. Termites and carpenter bees will eat your house. Normal wear and tear creates areas that look worn and torn, such as in front of the kitchen sink. Doorknobs become loose, and hinges squeak. Some things were simply not installed properly. All of these items are easy to fix if maintained, and none of them should be treated as if they'll fix themselves.

All houses have a warranty period. During this period, the house builder is responsible for items that are not installed properly or simply break. Even the best house builder cannot build a perfect house. However, all house builders should address the items in a house that are covered during the warranty period, and they should do it in a timely manner. The length and coverage of the house warranty should be agreed upon at the same time the contract for construction is finalized. The minimum warranty should be for a year; that's typical in the industry. Some builders offer longer warranties as a type of marketing edge. If things are not installed or built right or are defective, they will usually show up sooner than a year. If the new plumbing line in the wall behind the washing machine on the second floor springs a leak while you're out of town and floods the whole house, it would be a warranty item if it happened during the warranty period. If that old washing machine's water cutoff valve was worn out and the whole house flooded, that's not the contractor's fault. Hopefully, your homeowners insurance would cover that. Be sure you include a warranty and you understand what it covers before you sign the contract for your house construction.

There are some things that inherently require more maintenance than others. One is a swimming pool. I intentionally did not include a chapter on pools in this book because they're not worth the trouble to maintain them—that is, unless you're not doing it yourself. Before you have a pool built, ask anyone who has one, and also does his own maintenance, if he would do it again. Think of the initial cost, plus the monthly chemicals for black algae from hell, yellow mustard algae, chlorine, water purifiers, ph balancers, and the list goes on. Some people with pools have a sign that says, "I don't swim in your toilet, so don't pee in my pool." It's much easier and less expensive to join the local swim and racquet club near your house. Your kids will probably insist on going there to be with their friends anyway.

Take care of your house, and it will take care of you.

Conclusion

This book is the result of a lifetime of experiences in the construction industry with a major amount of the time associated with residential type construction. I have found that residential construction involves all aspects of the construction industry, from rough foundations to delicate finishes. Some buildings just have a floor and roof, such as a warehouse, some have a kitchen and dining room, some a garage and work areas, some sleeping rooms, some offices and meeting rooms, some gyms and bath rooms, and all the appliances and fixtures associated with those rooms. In residential construction, all of these areas in one way or another are condensed into a small project that's carefully inspected by the conscientious homeowner. You really have it all in a house.

Some say parts are parts, but you have to get all of these parts and the people involved with them to work in a synchronized order if you want the work to be of good quality and done as quickly as possible.

In construction, the one thing you do not want to happen is for the men and material to show up on the job site and nobody knows what to do. Or, the material shows up but no labor, or vice versa. Or, two trades show up and have to work in the same area. What this means, and I hope you derived this from the book, is that there's a lot of necessary planning and decision making prior to actually doing the work.

It does not take long to install a wireless doorbell, but someone has to pick out which kind, and someone has to decide where it goes by the door and if all the doors get them and if there will be different rings for different doors. These decisions should be made by the homeowner prior to the craftsmen who will actually do the work having to ask. These guys usually work by the hour and don't mind waiting all day while you decide. I know this is a simple example, but I see it happening on almost every job.

Spending the proper amount of time on the front side of the project is the key to keeping the project moving smoothly and on schedule. I believe it takes the same amount of time planning as it does constructing a custom house. The only difference is that the planning stages are considerably less expensive than the building stages. If you built the same house twice, you would see this quickly. You simply cannot build a house without plans—both drawn and written—and the better the plans are, the better and quicker the construction goes. Think of the contractor as the conductor to a full-blast orchestra and the sheet music as his plans. If a part of the sheet music is missing, the music stops until it's found. If the plans are complete, the music will sound like Elvis singing "Love Me Tender." If the plans are lousy, I don't even want to think about the pain that music would cause.

For some reason, contractors always seem to have a sense of urgency about them, as if they're constantly getting behind. That is not necessarily a bad trait unless that urgency is the result of bad planning. For example, the painter is ready to paint, but the colors have not been finalized. Whose fault would that be? Painting happens toward the end of the construction, so the impact wouldn't be that bad. But, consider an item that was critical in a sequence of construction that stopped all construction until that item was installed—something like a glue lam beam that you had to order and took two weeks to deliver. The beam supported a large part of the framing, so the framing stopped or went out of the logical productive path of construction along with all the other trades. Being urgent is necessary for things like flat tires, but otherwise it raises your blood pressure unnecessarily. When selecting a contractor, try to find one who is well organized. This would not be one who works out of his truck, unless his truck is like a Bradley mobile command station. I have found that the longer a contractor has been in business, the more organized he is.

Developing good plans and selecting the right contractor is all it takes to be able to enjoy watching your house being built. Take your time on both of those endeavors. I hope this book has provided you some insight into the land of construction and will prevent your experience there from being a struggle. If you keep your wits about you and do not let yourself get rushed into any decisions, I'm sure you will enjoy building your house. And, when the design professionals start to tell you about what's what, it won't be like you haven't heard it before.

One other thing, since I have to live with my Clemson buddies, and they don't like chickens and say derogatory things about them, here's to the great USC Gamecocks.

Until we meet in the big house in the sky, God bless and God speed with your next house.

Index

kitchen appliances, 95, 147–149, 147*ill*, 149*ill*

L
land surveyors, 9
    registered professional, 11
landscapers, 151–152
landscaping, 150–152, 150*ill*
lateral stability, 50
lath and grout beds in installing tiles, 119
lead in paint, 135–136
leaking pipes, 90
leaking roofs, 55
    due to penetrations, 63
legal description of property, 11
light switches and lights, 103–104
live loads
    building codes for floors, 113
    calculating, 21
    direction of pull, 23
    roof, 23, 53–54
load-bearing walls, 50
loads (forces)
    calculating, 21, 23
    dead, 21, 23
    differential settlements and, 25
    impact, 20
    live, 21, 23
    roof, 23
    seismic or earthquqke, 22–23
    wind, 22–23
louvers, 62–63
lumber
    costs associated with using, 46
    creep, 47
    cutting, 45
    for exterior wall finish, 51
    framing, 44–45
    grades of, 46
    moisture content, 47
    plywood, 45
    termites, 47

treated, 47

M
main front door, 68
main-floor plan, 58*ill*
maintenance and warranty, 156–158, 156*ill*
managing project, 158–161
mantles, 38
Masonite doors, 68
masonry, 31*ill*
    arches in, 36*ill*, 39–40
    basement options and precautions, 33–34
    cleaning, 35
    CMU, 32–33
    corbelling brickwork, 40
    cracks in, 75–76
    curtain walls, 32
    efflorescence, 40
    expansion coefficents for exterior siding, 76
    exterior siding using, 74–75
    exterior skin of house, 34
    grouting, 33
    hollow units, 33
    material, mortar as, 34–35
    mortar types, 35, 75
    muriatic acid wash, 35
    painting, 135
    poor workmanship, 40
    PSI rating for exterior siding, 75
    solid units, 33
    standard unit for, 32
    structures, 40–41
    ties, 34
    types of, 33
    waterproofing membrane, 40
masonry height to thickness ratio, exterior siding, 77
metal exterior siding, 74
metal roofs, 62